Social Media Marketing Secrets

The Latest Social Media Strategy For the Future on Instagram, Facebook, Youtube and Twitter, Advertising and Seo, Be an Influencer

Jack Gary

will be done as an illegal act regardless of the end form the information ultimately takes. This includes copied versions of the work both physical, digital and audio unless express consent of the Publisher is provided beforehand. Any additional rights reserved.

Furthermore, the information that can be found within the pages described forthwith shall be considered both accurate and truthful when it comes to the recounting of facts. As such, any use, correct or incorrect, of the provided information will render the Publisher free of responsibility as to the actions taken outside of their direct purview. Regardless, there are zero scenarios where the original author or the Publisher can be deemed liable in any fashion for any damages or hardships that may result from any of the information discussed herein.

Additionally, the information in the following pages is intended only for informational purposes and should thus be thought of as universal. As befitting its nature, it is presented without assurance regarding its prolonged validity or interim quality. Trademarks that are mentioned are done without written consent and can in no way be considered an endorsement from the trademark holder.

Table of Contents

other books By Jack Gary:

Facebook Advertising: The Ultimate Guide On Facebook ads and Tips to Succeed on Instagram, Youtube and Twitter, Advertise your Brand Grow your Social Media

Instagram Marketing 2019: Secrets to Growth Your Brand

Personal Branding in 2019: Strategies to Build Your Brand With Instagram, Facebook, Youtube and Twitter, Social Media Marketing and Network Marketing

Introduction

The following chapters will discuss everything that you need to know in order to find the right social media platform to promote your business and how to make it as successful as possible. Social media has taken over the world. Your customers are already online, looking for their news, their favorite businesses, and more. As a business, it is important to create your own presence online so you can meet your customers where they need you most.

This guidebook is going to take time to look at all of the secrets and tips that you need to know to get started with your own social media marketing campaign. We are going to look at the top social media platforms including Facebook, Twitter, Instagram, and YouTube. Each of these social media platforms is full of benefits, and they can ensure that you meet your customer in the right place at the right time.

Building up a presence online and making sure that you provide useful and valuable content to your customers can be hard. And choosing which social media site and platform to go with may seem almost impossible. This guidebook will delve into each of the social media sites and discuss the best marketing strategies to make each one work. Whether you are looking to work with Instagram, Facebook, Twitter, or YouTube, or some combination of them, you will be able to use this guidebook to help you get started.

There are many different aspects that you have to consider when it is time to start your own marketing campaign, but you can't forget to include your online presence and your presence on social media. Make sure to check out this guidebook to learn everything that you need to know to get started with your social media marketing plan.

Chapter 1: The Influence of Social Media

As a business, if you are not on a social media account yet, or preferably several of them, then it is time to get started right away. Social media has taken over the world. Your friends are on it, your customers are on it, and your competition is already on it. Social media allows you to reach your customers in a more interactive way than ever before. And any business can benefit from having a profile and meeting with their customers online on a regular basis.

Your business needs to have a social media presence. It is the best way to interact with your customers, to talk to them and build up trust, to beat out your competition, to tell more about your company, and to make yourself more visible on search engines. Let's take some time to look at the big influence of social media online and some of the benefits and reasons why you should have a social media marketing strategy prepared right away.

Search Engine Visibility

Every business wants to be able to increase the amount of user engagement and traffic that they have. But, is it really possible to do all of this if your potential customers aren't even able to find you when they go online? There are a number of ways that you can increase the potential customers to your site, but having a good social media profile can help you dominate those first search result pages in a natural and organic way. And this, in turn, increases the profits that you earn.

When you are thinking about this, you can consider the fact that millennials already spend a ton of time on social platforms, and having your own is going to increase the value of your company more than ever. It can not only help you to generate more business and profits for yourself, but it can also stop some of the brand negativity it takes to reach top positions.

The Mouthpiece for Your Company

Whether you have been in the industry for a long time or you are new to the industry, having a positive word of mouth for your business will help you to gain more customers to keep your business running. Social media marketing can be a great way to help you as a business owner interact with your customers and spread more good word of mouth. You can use it to talk about policies in the company, team activities, new launches, and any other information that is needed for the business.

Social networking online can really help your business because you are given a chance to build up a narration that you can use to capture the interest of your customers. Each post that you do on Facebook and each tweet on Twitter can share the values and ethics of the company, along with the product, and can go so far in promoting you and your business.

One thing to keep in mind here is that, while social media can be a great mouthpiece for your company, that doesn't mean that you should flood everyone with a ton of posts all the time. Writing a post twenty times a day is going to get excessive and will annoy your customers. Posting a few times is fine, but make sure that everything you post is relevant and will provide some value to your customers.

Can Build up Trust with Your Customers

No matter where you advertise to your customers, whether it is online or not, you will find that you have to build up trust with your customers or they are never going to choose your products over the competition. This is even more important when it comes to social media because you don't get a chance for the customer to come and meet up with you—they have to do it all online.

Social media and the presence that you can build upon there has become so important when it comes to earning the trust of your customer. You can make your business and see it survive without needing a physical store. But, without a good presence on social media, your customers won't know who you are and they may not even give you a chance.

Provides You with a Competitive Advantage

Take a look at some of the things that your competitors are doing. How many of them are finding social media as a good way to reach their own customers. Do you think that your competitors thought it was smart to ignore social media and stay off of it? You are going to be wrong on this one. There is a big chance that your competitors are already investing both their money and their time on at least a few social media sites in the hope of making a positive presence and gaining business. If you aren't doing this and you aren't willing to learn how to do this, then you are going to be at a big disadvantage.

You will find that not giving your business a good presence on social media means that you are missing out on all of the good benefits that come from these platforms. And when you pass on the benefits, this automatically benefits your competition more. So, it may be a good idea to check into social media and see what it can do for you.

Virtually Connect with Your Customers

When you aren't able to meet with your customer face to face, it is sometimes hard to convince them that your product is the best one for them to go with. It is critical that as a virtual company, one who sells their items online and tries to market and sell products online, that you can prove your credibility and gain the confidence and trust from your customers.

You will quickly find that these social media platforms are going to give you the opportunity to create a good bond with your customers. Your brand has to know that it is so important to engage with your customers, and using social media can be one of the best ways to help promote your services. You can showcase the products you have, give testimonies, and even interact with customers so that they have a chance to engage with your business any time that they want.

The Best Business and Sales Leads

One of the main reasons that a lot of companies choose to go on social media is to help them generate leads, and social media can do wonders for making this happen. And with the help of some social media channels like YouTube and Pinterest, which allow direct purchases, the game of social media is even more powerful than before. Instagram has even jumped on board with this new trend and launched their own call to action button, one that is going to help its audience to shop and install any application that it needs.

This makes it easier for your business to reach your customers. With interactive posts and lots of pictures to showcase your products and services, you can really reach customers and even make the sale. The added bonus comes when you can have a little 'Buy Now' button on your post so customers don't have to search around in order to purchase any item they want, making things easier than ever.

The world of social media is evolving and changing very fast, and it is going to help you drive sales in a big way. If you don't make this a part of your marketing strategy and work to sell your products there, then it is going to be very hard for you to beat out the competition.

A Good Marketing Channel

As a business, you want to make sure that you can drive sales well. This is one of the biggest merits that come from using a social network site. All of the various channels of social media that you will use have their own marketing machinery in place. Each of them works in slightly different ways, but these marketing options are going to make it easier for your brand to connect with the audience that you are targeting. For example, the Sponsored Posts from Facebook and Twitter's Marketing Campaign are two of the most popular ways to market your products and services.

One of the nice things that you will find with a variety of social media channels is that they have their own unique marketing options. They have developed their marketing options in order to improve the reach that you can make with your audience. Though you don't always need to have a good presence in social media to use these channels, but it can help. Many global brands link a lot of their marketing campaigns with the social profiles that they create to increase both likes and followers.

If your business hasn't been able to get into social media yet, the time is now. The power that comes with social media is huge, and you will be amazed at the number of doors that it can open up to bring more success to your business, as long as you use it in the right manner. Benefits that are generated by various social media channels are measurable and so many companies have the results behind them, therefore, there really isn't a reason that you shouldn't take advantage of it as well.

There are a lot of benefits of using social media and getting the most out of using it. There are a ton of different sites out there that you can choose from, and you are sure to enjoy the different options as they help you reach your overall goals. You have to be careful about choosing the right social channels and make sure that you have a detailed strategy in order to make this all work.

Just posting some images on occasion and doing status updates is not going to be enough to help you run your business. Finding the right combination of informative and promotion posts and targeting your posts to meet with your audience are required in order to generate the desired results. In addition, being able to generate the leads that your business needs from advertising on social media can be a new ballgame which can really help your business to grow.

Why Is Social Media so Important for My Business?

We are going to spend some time in this guidebook talking about social media and the different ways you can use it to help promote your business. But why should you consider using social media? Isn't the marketing plan that you already have working well, and isn't it enough to help you grow your business?

There are many other ways that you can market your business and still reach your potential customers. You can work with radio and television advertisements. You can work with an email campaign. You can send out fliers, work with putting ads up online, and so much more. And all of these should be considered when you are working on your own marketing plan.

But, if you choose to ignore the power of social media, you are really leaving something important on the table. Social media can get you in touch with your customers, right where they are. Most of the advertising that you will do on social media is very affordable, especially when you compare what you get out of it; it is very cost efficient. When you want to make sure that your budget can last as long as possible, then working with Facebook, Instagram, YouTube, and Twitter can be one of the best ways to do it.

Another benefit is that you are going to see some great results when you try to personalize yourself with the customer. There are a lot of different companies out there for your customers to choose from. If they don't see your personality and what sets you apart from others, then they won't really have a reason to choose you over someone else. Using social media to open up and really showcase your business can be a fantastic way to seem more personal with your customers, and it can help you get more profits in the long run.

Your customers are already on social media; they are there in large numbers and ready to spend their money. This alone should be enough reason to get you to consider advertising your business through social media. If you pick out the right platform and learn how to use it in the most optimal and efficient manner, you can reach your customers right where they are, and this alone can do wonders for helping you see amazing results with the growth of your business.

And finally, if you don't take advantage of social media, then your competition will. Do you really want to give your competition a leg up on you simply because you refuse to be on social media, and at least use it a bit in your marketing plan? Your competition is already working closely with one or more social media sites, interacting with their customers and trying to gain more business. If you want to get a piece of the pie, then you need to do the same.

Social media, whether you use Facebook, Twitter, YouTube, or Instagram, can be a great way to grow your business, to make sure that your reputation is doing well, and so much more. You will be able to pick out which one will work the best for you based on the type of customer you work with, the product that you sell, and more. Make sure to check out the other chapters in this guidebook to help you learn more about each social media site and how you can use each one to help promote your business.

Chapter 2: YouTube, Facebook, Instagram, and Twitter — How Each Works and Which One Is Right for You

There are a lot of social media platforms out there. Some platforms cater to a certain demographic, and others are there to reach the customer as a whole. There are too many of these platforms to spend time on, so in this chapter, and the rest of the book, we are going to focus mainly on looking at the four big names, YouTube, Facebook, Instagram, and Twitter, to get an idea of how they work and who will benefit from each one the most.

One note here is that while all of these social media platforms have a huge reach and lots of potential customers, not all of them may be right for you. Depending on the business you are in and where your customers are at, you may have to limit yourself to just using one or two. You also have to be careful about not spreading yourself out too thin. It is easy to agree to work on ten social media sites and then feel overwhelmed by the work that needs to be done. If you only choose one or two social media sites to work on, you will find it is much more effective compared to not being able to keep up with a bunch of them.

Let's take a look at the top four social media platforms for your business and get a good idea of which one is the right one for you.

YouTube

YouTube is the first platform that we are going to take a look at. This one is often not seen as a social media platform because it doesn't meet some of the traditional outlines that the others do. But making videos and posts for your customers on this platform will help you to grow your business. Creating videos takes some more time compared to just writing out a quick post, but it can really make a difference in the reach that you can get to your customers.

The first question here is why you should consider marketing on YouTube. There are a lot of benefits that come with marketing on YouTube that many businesses don't consider fully. The first is that video is a huge thing right now. It is actually taking over the world of marketing, and if you aren't using a video, you are going to find that the competition is already ahead of you. And this isn't a joke. Video ranks higher on all of the social platforms out there, which means that customers are more likely to notice and respond to businesses that use a video compared to those that just do a regular post.

When you decide to use the YouTube platform, you are going to have a big library of videos that you can use. You can choose to go through and upload your video files natively to every platform. Or, there is the option to embed the videos into your blog posts, just with a few clicks, which can help you to make the blog posts more engaging and dynamic.

Another benefit is that YouTube already has a very big and diverse audience and many of the people in that audience are going to work with both the search engine on Google and YouTube to help them find any content that they want. If you are good at optimizing your keywords to go along with the videos, you will be able to have an instant connection with your audience, rather than hoping that the right ads on Facebook will show up on the newsfeeds for your customers.

Any business who decides to work with YouTube will find that they have a large potential audience group that they can work with. You just have to find ways to make high-quality videos and use the right keywords so you can reach those customers and get them to make a purchase. Add in that these videos from YouTube can also show up near the top of search results for Google, this can make it easier for your customers to find the videos that you are posting.

And the final benefit is that there are not that many businesses that are using YouTube right now. While you can go online and find so many videos, only about 9% of small businesses are using YouTube. This means that you will gain an edge over the competition because there isn't as much found on this platform. If you can create high-quality and entertaining videos, you could easily get in early and beat out the competition, resulting in more sales along the way.

To really see some success when you get started with YouTube, you must ensure that your approach is different than what you see on other social media platforms. The other options that we will talk about will revolve around the idea of creating and sharing great content with the goal of creating conversation, engagement, and awareness. This is basically all about socializing online.

But with YouTube, things are a bit different. These videos that you will post are more similar to blog posts than anything else, and they are going to fit in more effectively to content marketing. Yes, there are times when people will comment, but these comments are going to be similar to the way they comment on a blog post, not an active discussion like we see on other posts. Your customers are going to come to your profile to view and digest videos, rather than share their thoughts about the day. This is why any marketing that you do on YouTube should be seen more as content marketing rather than social media marketing.

Some of the key points that you should remember when working with marketing your business on YouTube include:

1. People who find your videos on YouTube are going to find them when doing a search or when they view other content that is related. On most social media sites, outside of Pinterest, they may see you if they follow you, if they see your information from ads, or if one of their friends engaged with you.

2. The emphasis that comes with YouTube is to watch videos, not spend time discussing them. You don't really see a lot of people tagging others when they do comment like they might in other sites. Remember that YouTube is more about the experience of the viewer, rather than a social one. If someone wants to, they will decide to share it on the platform of their choice.

3. Many people are going to come to YouTube because their intention is to sit down and watch a video. They probably won't get there and idly scroll through the feed like they might with Facebook.

When you learn how to approach your YouTube

channel as a platform with good content, rather than a social one, you will find that it is easier to create stronger videos, ones that your potential customers will like and ones that can perform well.

Facebook

The next social media platform that you may want to take a look at is Facebook. Facebook has been the leader in social media for many years now, and it is often the first place that businesses are going to look when it is time to promote their businesses. They know that there are a ton of customers on the page, and if they use insightful and useful posts along the way, they will be able to reach their target audience.

Facebook is still one of the largest social media platforms out there, and this is naturally one of the first places that a lot of companies choose to go with. You will be able to reach a lot of customers, and Facebook has a variety of options available to you to help reach your customers. You can choose to set up a business page where you can interact with your customers, share information, and discuss things with them.

You have the option of doing a classic ad, do a promotion, promote one of the posts that you put on one of your pages, do a sponsored page or past, work with an open graph to help you label the actions of your users and learn more about them, and so much more. No social media site has as many options as Facebook, which is part of why it is such a great social media platform for you to choose to work with.

There are also a lot of advertising features that you can use when you decide to use Facebook as your main social media platform. Some of the features that you will be able to see when you use Facebook advertising include:

- Built-in ad performance measurement tools
- Ad testing, which means that you can send out several versions of an ad at the same time for you to compare which one works the best before deciding
- The ability to set up the budget you want to work with when you send out an ad
- Help with demographic targeting based on interests, education, location, and age

What this means is that Facebook has a lot of the tools and features that you can look for in order to improve your business and to target your customers. You can measure how an ad is doing, check and see which version out of several ads seems to have the best response, and so much more.

Not everyone is going to see some benefits when they go with Facebook. While there are a lot of benefits and Facebook can provide you with the audience and the tools that you need to really see your business grow, you will find that, sometimes, it isn't right. Don't just go right into marketing on Facebook just because it is the biggest name out there, unless you know for sure that you will be able to reach your audience. Depending on the type of business you are and the products you sell, it may be more efficient to work with a different platform.

This isn't to turn you from Facebook. Many companies will still choose to go with Facebook because of all it has to offer. But Facebook doesn't have every audience out there, and it can get expensive, especially if you aren't even reaching the right customers. Doing your research ahead of time ensures that you are reaching your customers and choosing Facebook because it is the right option, not just because everyone else is doing it.

Instagram

The next option that you can choose to work with when it is time to promote your business is Instagram. Instagram is quickly growing in popularity, and with all of the great features, such as a 'Buy Now' button that you can add into your posts, it is easy to see why so many people want to move into advertising and marketing through Instagram.

Instagram is a picture-sharing site. It works similarly to other social media sites, but for this one, you are going to focus your energy on providing high-quality pictures first, and then good descriptions second. The first thing people are going to notice when they come to your Instagram profile is the pictures that you have. Everything is about pictures, and if you put ones up that don't relate to your business or you pick out ones that aren't high-quality, then customers are going to turn away, and you will never see results.

31

It has become clear recently that Instagram isn't just a site for personal use. It is a global platform that makes it easier for companies and various brands that humanize their content, showcases all of their products, recruit the new talent that they need, and even to inspire their audience. And all of these can be done with the right pictures that show up on your page.

The nice thing that happens with the users of Instagram is that they just aren't active, but they also engage with you. This video and picture sharing app is now becoming one of the top sites for social media. In fact, over half of the active users on the site are on it each day, and 35% of those say that they check the account for more than one time a day.

What this means is that there is a huge amount of potential for your business to grow through this platform. Instagram is a good way to introduce some of your products and can make it easier to grow more brand awareness. In fact, research has shown that at least 70% of users on Instagram have spent some time looking up a brand on that specific social media platform.

Instagram allows you to promote your brand and your product in a way that is authentic and friendly, without having to focus on using hard selling tactics that never work and can turn your customers off from the product. If you can provide high-quality products to your customers and can even share some good videos, you will find that Instagram may be the social media site that works the best for you.

You will find that many businesses are starting to move over to Instagram as a way to promote their business. But, it is still relatively new and there is a lot of room for your business to grow. We will discuss some of the different ways that you can really promote yourself on this social site, but providing high-quality pictures, interacting with your customers, and playing around with different hashtags and timings for the posts can make a difference in the results that you can get with this platform.

Twitter

And finally, we need to take a look at Twitter and what it can do for your business. Twitter currently has more than 313 million monthly active users, and most of the demographic are younger, which makes it perfect for most marketers and businesses. Getting started on Twitter is pretty easy as well because anyone can pick out the right Twitter handle, upload a profile picture, fill out the bio, and then send out a tweet or two. The issue that comes up is learning how to grow the account and how to turn it into a tool that will build your brand and bring in leads.

You will quickly find that growing the type of customer base that you want with Twitter is going to take a bit more than sending out tweets only when the company has a big event or when a new product is being released. It is more about engaging with your target audience and then finding ways to interact with them in meaningful and valuable ways.

The first question that you may have when it comes to Twitter is: how this social media site is different from the other options that we have talked about so far? Understanding the way that Twitter works, especially when compared to other social media sites, can ensure that you get the most out of your Twitter marketing plan.

34

There are actually a lot of different ways that businesses use Twitter to help with their marketing and some of these include:

- Managing their reputation
- Branding
- Networking
- Letting them interact with their customers
- Driving engagement for promotional activities
- Sharing information and content

Most of these have something to do with your interactions and how you get along with the customers you have. It is not all about broadcasting your content, like what you will see with Pinterest. Twitter is more about communication and keeping those lines open with your customer.

If you are looking for a different way to meet with your customers and to have more communication and interaction with them compared to some of the other sites, then Twitter is the right option for you. Twitter has so many different options that you can choose to go with to help you market, and it has changed so much in the past few years to include more services and more neat things to help you grow your business.

Twitter is a bit different compared to some of the other platforms. It is more about opening up a conversation with your customer, something that can be done with the other options, but isn't always done. If you can open up the lines of communication with your customer and you are ready to have a conversation with your customers, you will find that Twitter is the best social media platform for you.

Which One Should I Choose to Work With?

As you can see, all of the social media platforms that we have talked about can be a great way to promote your business. They provide so many options to choose from and so many ways that you can interact with your customers. But spreading yourself out to so many different areas can be hard to do. Most marketing plans need to have a solid focus on just one or two social media platforms to ensure they can reach their customers in the right place, without wasting time, effort, and money. So, how do you choose the right one for you?

The answer really depends on the kind of business you run and how you think you can really beat out your competition. Going where the customers actually are and meeting them in a new and innovative way, rather than just following the competition or picking one because it sounds neat, is the best way to make sure that you pick out the right social media site.

If you know that most of your target audience is on Facebook, and you think you can interact and get in contact with them the easiest that way, then this is the method that you should use. But if you find that videos may be the best way to showcase your products or could be a better way to reach your customers that the competition hasn't gotten to yet, then YouTube may be a good option.

For those companies that know a picture is worth a thousand words and who have a ton of great products that would look amazing in pictures, then Instagram may be a good option. Or, if you want to really open up communication with your customers and want to work on building up your reputation online, then Twitter may be the way to go.

When you are first getting started with your social media marketing campaign, make sure that you pick just one or two to start with. This allows you to get really familiar with the audience on there and the way the platform works. You can always add in more sites later on and even drop some if you want, but starting out with a few can be the best use of your budget money and ensures you really get a chance to use them properly before adding in more.

Chapter 3: Facebook and Your Business

Facebook is one of the biggest social media platforms out there. Everyone has heard of Facebook, and many people have a personal profile to help them connect with others, look at the news, and even follow some of their favorite companies. While you may use Facebook with a business page and in a different manner than your customer, it is still a great way for you to connect with customers and lead to sales.

Let's take a closer look at Facebook and some of the reasons that your business needs to consider setting up a presence organically on this social media site.

Why Is Facebook Important for Your Business?

Facebook is one of the largest social media sites out there. Almost everyone you talk to is going to agree that they have a Facebook account and that they use it on a regular basis, most people are on at least one time each day. This means that there is a huge pool of current and potential customers on this site that you can reach, resulting in most sales than ever. While it is going to take some creativity to find ways to reach out to your customers in a new and innovative way that others haven't already done, there is still a lot of great reasons to choose to go with Facebook for your business.

There are a lot of different parts of Facebook, and businesses that can learn about and understand how this system works the best are the ones that get ahead. Some of the things that you need to know about Facebook and why it is so important to use it in your own marketing campaigns and plans includes:

1. *There are more than 400 million users around the world*: Facebook has recently announced that it passed the mark for 400 million members. This means that if Facebook were a country, it would be the third largest in the world. Think of all the potential customers you can reach here.

2. *100 million users from the U.S.*: Out of the numbers that we listed above, 100 million of those users come from the United States. This is a huge target audience for you to use, even here in the United States.

3. *The average user spends 55 minutes on this site each day*: This is almost an hour a day. This is a lot of time to spend on Facebook, which gives you plenty of opportunities to reach out to your customer and get them to look into your products.

4. *80,000 sites are working with Facebook Connect*: Connect is an initiative through Facebook that has the greatest long-range impact. By integrating with Facebook closely, sites are making social graphs easier to use and more portable. Instead of heading to Facebook and other sites to visit with friends, the participants can travel with Facebook and see what is going on at all times. Even sites like Myspace and Yahoo! are starting to come in with these integrations.

5. *The average user on Facebook has 130 friends*: This means that you have a lot of room to grow your business. If you can get just one person interested in your products, they may be willing to share their love of the product with their friends. This is an extra 130 impressions that you can earn.

6. *The average user on Facebook will become a fan of four pages each month*: If you think that your customers are quickly going to become big fans of the Facebook page that you set up for the company without doing much work, then you have to pull back a bit on your expectations for the work. The average user is only going to become a fan of four pages each month. This isn't a ton considering how many different organizations, causes, and brands we are in contact with on a regular basis.

7. *The wall posts you have won't impact popularity*: A study that was done by Sysomos found that there isn't really much correlation between how often you post on the wall and how many fans there are. However, there is a

strong connection between the amount of other content, such as videos, photos, links, and notes, and how many fans you have. If you want to work with Facebook and you are looking to increase your fan base so you can reach more people, it is important that you move yourself beyond the simple wall posts. Adding in things like links, videos, and photos, to name a few, can help you out.

8. *Facebook has a customized News Feed*: Facebook recently made a move to an algorithm-driven news feed. What this means is that just because someone has become your fan, it doesn't mean they are going to always see your status updates or wall posts. This is true when we look at business and individual posts. Instead, the news feed is going to be set on default based on the content Facebook things you will lack. This is all based on interactions with content from the author in the past and interactions by your friends on that content.

This can put a lot of premium on posting content that is more engaging and will be more likely to get the shares, comments, and likes that you want. If you are not already paying attention to the analytics you get from Facebook, then now is the time to do so. You can look at your engagement scores and then mess around with some different types of content to see what would work the best for you.

There are many reasons why you should choose to work with Facebook as part of your marketing campaign. It is one of the largest platforms for social media right now, meaning that you get the benefit of reaching a ton of potential customers in an organic way. You also have a ton of options when it comes to advertising with Facebook, with many tools that Facebook has set up specifically to handle all of your business needs.

Now, if you are looking to get your business up and running on Facebook, you must first set up your own business page. This is relatively simple to do. Facebook will ask you a few questions, and then you can go in and fill out the rest of the parts and the rest of the sections. Make sure you provide a link to your website, add in some pictures, and fill in the About Me section. If you have a physical location as well, it is a good idea to add this into the page. The more complete the page is, the better things will be, whether you use organic or paid reach to get customers there.

It is also a good idea to spend your time writing out a few posts. No customer wants to come to your business page and see nothing there. Even as a beginner, get into the habit of posting on a regular basis. There might not be a ton of customers in the beginning, but it won't take long before more show up, and they will have a much better time interacting with you if they see there is already a lot of content there.

Organic Ways to Grow with Facebook

When it comes to advertising on Facebook or on any other site that you choose to use, you have two options: you can choose to grow your reach organically or with paid advertising. Growing your reach organically can be a nice method to use because you are surer that the customers who come to you really want your products or your information. And most organic methods are cheap or free so it helps your budget. However, these methods are much slower than what you can get with an advertisement, and you will find that it can take several months to several years to get the same reach organically as you can with paid advertising, especially when you are on Facebook.

With that said, it is best if you can do some combination of the two options. Organic reach can still be done, even if you are still using paid advertising to get the customers to you. In fact, this can help you get the most results for the least amount of money overall. Let's take a look at some of the steps you can take in order to organically grow your own business with the help of Facebook.

There are many things that you can do in order to grow the organic reach that you want when you are on Facebook. Keep in mind that this organic reach is often going to be at a slower pace than you may want, but it can build up some really great customers, the ones who are actually interested in your product, who may already be searching for your product, and who may be more willing to share the posts that you have. Some of the best things that you can do to increase your organic reach on Facebook include:

- *Build up your authority and your presence*: Your customers are going to come to you because they think you are the expert or the authority on a topic. Taking the time to show this in your posts and the items that you put on your business page can go a long way in bringing in more customers and keeping them around.

- *Make sure that your content is evergreen*: An evergreen content is a content that isn't going to be out-of-date in a few weeks, months, or even years. This is a content that can provide value to your customers and will serve them well whether they look at the information right then or they look at it a few weeks down the road. Sure, it is fine to have a limited time promotion for your business on occasion, but the majority of the content that you place on your profile or your business page should be evergreen for your customers.

- *Post when the competition is sleeping*: There can be a lot of noise on Facebook if you are not careful. Instead of going through and posting when all of your competition does and risk being drowned out by it all if you can do so and you notice that your customers are still responding well, try to post at times when the competition is pretty quiet. This ensures that you get to be front and center, without any other noise in the process.

- *Test how often you should post for the best results*: There is a lot of advice out there on how many times you should post, and even when you should put your posts up on a Facebook business page. But the trick here is to find the time that seems to work the best for your customers, and then do your posting there. This will help you to reach your customers where they are, whether it is in the morning, afternoon, or night. Some companies may find that they need to post more often, while some may only need to post once or twice a day. Look through your Facebook analytics and determine the right times for you to do your posting.

- *Let your email list do some of the work*: If your business has been growing for some time, then you may already have a good email list that you could try out. This email list can be used for a variety of things, but one option is to promote your Facebook page a little bit. This doesn't have to be done all the time, but letting your email list customers know that you have this page and that they can get exciting updates on there, can be a good way to get more people to follow you on Facebook.

- *Run a contest*: Nothing is better to organically grow your customer base than running a contest. You can choose the method you want to use to run this contest, but make sure that the incentive is one that will get other people to pay attention to what you are offering. You can use this to get more sales, to get more followers, or for a combination of the two.

- *Use copy that is persuasive and will grab attention*: The copy that you write on your business page is going to be so important when it comes to how much attention you will get from your customers. You want a copy that is friendly, persuasive, and will grab the attention of your customers. When it comes to advertising on Facebook, remember that your customers may see hundreds of posts a day. You must find some way to stand out from the crowd.

- *If you are going to use hashtags, use them in the proper manner*: Hashtags can be used on Facebook, even though they are most commonly used with Twitter. But you shouldn't just use a hashtag just because the option is there. You need to be strategic about the way that you use these hashtags. Pick out ones that are unique, ones that go with your business name or ones that your customers are more likely to look for when they want to find your business.

- *Make sure that you focus more on providing value than on your reach*: Sometimes, we get so caught up in trying to get more reach, and our content is going to suffer. Poor content on the business page is not going to keep your current customers around, and it definitely won't bring in any new potential customers either. Make sure that you focus your attention on providing value to your customers, and the rest will take care of itself.

No matter what plan you choose to go with for your Facebook marketing campaign, make sure that you include at least a few of these tips for growing the page organically. Even when it comes to some of the paid advertising that you want to do, things like evergreen content, and providing some kind of value to your customers can not only help increase your organic reach but can also make your advertising more effective.

Chapter 4: Facebook Marketing

While you will want to take some time to work through some of the steps to organically grow your content, like what we talked about previously, many companies have started to look towards Facebook advertising in order to help them. Finding all of the customers that you need can be hard, especially when you consider how much competition and noise is already on the social media site. Working with paid advertising can actually make a big difference because it allows you to get your ads right in front of your target audience when you need it the most.

Facebook makes it easy for you to create your very own ads. You can choose to release just one ad, do an A/B testing to see how each one works, and then pick and more. Facebook even makes it easy for you to pick out a whole campaign so you can get the most out of your work and budget. Let's take a look at some of the steps that you can take to create your own ad for Facebook and how to get the most out of your budget when you decide to do   paid advertising.

Choose What You Want to Promote

This is going to be different for everyone involved. Some people want to be able to promote their business and just increase brand awareness. Some people want to increase their reach and will advertise in this manner. And, still, others may choose that they want to sell a new product or a campaign of products and increase their sales.

You can choose any of these categories that you want and more, but you have to come up with a clear idea of what it is before you even start. Each of these categories will require different things to occur, and they will each shape what is going on with your campaign and the decisions that you make. Facebook helps with this because it will provide you with the opportunity to promote your Facebook place or page or an external URL, such as your website. You just have to choose which one you want.

Choose the Objective of the Ad

Now, it is time to get down to the nitty-gritty and determine what the objective of the ad should be. Are you looking to see if you can increase the number of likes that you can get on the page? Are you looking to promote a particular post in order to get more views and maybe more purchases?

Many businesses are going to work to promote a post. This allows them to get some more likes on a page and more eyes paying attention to them. And in many cases, the post is set up to help advertise the business or a particular product that they are trying to sell to their customers.

Another thing that you can try out is to promote a post that can link back to a particular blog article for your business (if you don't already have a blog up and running, it is time to get it done), and this would then lead the customer to a landing page to help with lead generation.

Create the Ad That You Want to Promote

From here, we need to go through and actually create the ad that our potential customers are going to see on their news feed. If you have never gone through and done this process in the past, it can seem a bit daunting. But Facebook has things set up to make it easier for you; you simply need to follow the right steps, and you will be fine.

First, let's look at what you need to do if you plan on using this advertisement to promote your own page. To do this you need to work with the following:

- Upload an image that is at least 100 px by 72 px. This is often going to be your logo, but you can also choose another image that fits your needs or the needs of the advertisement. Make sure that it is high-quality and will actually help promote your business.

- Create a headline. If you are just trying to promote your own page, then Facebook will go through and do this for you. When Facebook puts this information in, it is going to be the company name that was added into your file.

- Now, you need to create the ad text. You are given 90 characters to write out a small description of your business. You can either write out your own and make it persuasive and catchy or the default is the description for your business that you wrote on your page.

If you want to promote a post instead, the ad that you are doing will simply hold the post of your choice. It is as simple as that!

Target the Ad

One of the most important decisions that you will make when it comes to your ad and your promotion is how to target it. It is a huge waste of money if you just send out the ad with a bunch of guesses because you are likely to send it to the wrong demographics. Basically, you need to know your audience, what they like to do, and where to reach them.

If you don't already know your target audience, then it is time to get to work. You are going to just waste your time and money if you don't have this information, so get together with your marketing team and figure it out. Once that is done, you will be better prepared to target your ad to the right people.

Facebook will provide you with four ways to segment out your audience. These will include:

- Target by the geographic location: You get the choice to target your ad based on the country, state, city, zip code, and more of your customer.

- You can target by the age or the gender.

- It is possible to go through and target by interest. This is where you are able to segment out your advertising in order to pinpoint the audience that you would like to reach. For example, if you are running a specialty running store, you would choose some interests like exercise, fitness, marathons, and running. Then, you would make sure that with this segmentation that your add is only going to show up to those who have already shown themselves interested in the topics that you chose.

- Target by the connection status. For this one, you will choose to show your ad to the individuals who are already connected to your page.

Set the Budget

Facebook also allows you to be in full control over the budget that you work with. You can set a daily budget that you want to stick with for each day of the campaign or a total campaign budget for Facebook to work with. If you are just starting out with this, it is a good idea to do a smaller budget, and then as you optimize the strategy that you are using with advertising, you can spend more on the budget.

One thing to note with the budget on Facebook is that it is set so that the ad is going to run continuously. Make sure that you go through and add a start date and an end date to this ad. This helps you to be more in control over how long the advertisement is going to run with. As a beginner, you may find that a smaller campaign that runs for 7 days and has a budget of $10 a day is a good place to start.

When you are setting the budget up, you can choose to be charged with a cost per impression or a cost per click depending on your overall goals. If you are trying to promote your page and you want to get the maximum amount of page likes possible, the default charge is going to be charged each time that someone sees the ad within the defined target audience, which means you are being charged a cost per impression. If you are trying to promote a post that will link back to your website, then the default is to charge you cost per click, which means that you will only be charged when someone actually clicks on your ad and is redirected to your posts.

Also, Facebook may have times when it goes slightly over your budget if it thinks that it can really use the money to promote better on one day or another. This means that the daily budget will be taken a bit over, but your campaign budget will still end up the same; one of the other days will just get a bit less money. So, if you are doing a campaign that is $10 a day for 7 days, you will still spend only $70 on the campaign, but you may spend $15 on a day and $7 on a couple other days to cover it.

Measure the Results and Learn How to Optimize Your Ads

It is never a good idea to place an ad or promotion on Facebook and just ignore it. Many people forget that they should use some of the analytic tools that are available through Facebook to help them make smart decisions about their business and to help them to optimize their ads so they get the most out of the process.

You can use Facebook analytics to help you do this. This analytics help you to see how much you spent, which days you spent the most, how your customer seemed to react to the work that you were doing, and more. There are a lot of insights that you can get when it comes to working with this analytics, and you are really just harming your own business if you aren't willing to look at them. These insights can give you a lot of information on how to improve and make your future ads so much better.

Running an A/B Test

One option that you may want to consider when it comes to your Facebook page is running A/B testing. What this includes is taking two ads that are pretty similar, but with little differences in them. You may use this when you have two ads that may be really good, and you want to see which one would do the best. You would work on both of the ads, and then send them out at the same time to see how customers respond.

The budget for each ad has to be the same, and they are usually pretty small because you are doing a small test run. You can then watch the analytics on each one and determine which one is sticking around and which is going to be your main campaign. This is a great way to reserve your budget while also reducing your risk because you know exactly which advertisement your customers will respond to the best.

Using the Idea of Geo-Targeting

This is a way to pin a certain audience for a specific geographic. This is one of the most direct ways to direct your message and a very effective and powerful to boost your efficacy. With just a few clicks on Facebook, you have a new ad that's ready for advertising. But, of course, there's a catch—there is no easy route when conducting business. Taking this route can really jack up the price of your campaign.

Attracting higher value customers, businesses can benefit from this method whether it's a real estate company looking for a higher source or a B2B business looking to amplify a higher average to attract new business that will pay more for the growth of the company.

Your business can use this method to help them find some new customers. You can place your physical location and then make advertisements to local customers. With regular outbound sales, this process could cost you thousands of dollars. But Facebook Ads can do the work for you without all the hassle.

In order to target the group that you want, you can just set up an ad with Facebook as usual. When you get to the audience, you can drop a pin in the area where you are located. This shows the program where you are located and that you want to reach other customers in the same area. After you have dropped the pin, make sure to work with the radius slider. This lets you pick how far away you want customers from this area.

So, if you want to reach customers that are within an hour of your location, you can move the slider bar to 60 miles out. This ensures that you get the best possible reach with this feature.

Organic vs. Paid Marketing on Facebook

So far, we have spent some time talking about both organic and paid advertising on Facebook and how you can use each one. But which of these methods is actually the best one to work with?

In reality, you will need to work with both of these together to see the best results. Organic is usually the best method. This allows you to bring a lot of value to your customers, providing them with posts and information that they can actually use. And the customers who end up on your page are individuals who actually want to be there and who are interested in hearing more from you.

But there is just so much noise and competition out there, and it is hard to be heard above it all with just organic reach. Paid advertising, especially with Facebook, can help you to reach the group that you want without getting drowned out. But you need to have a good organic reach, with lots of good content, before you can even make this happen.

Chapter 5: Instagram Marketing and Techniques

Instagram can be a very big mystery for a lot of companies. They want to be able to reach their target audience, and they know that working with Instagram can be the best way to make this happen in some cases. But they also may not be sure how to get started with Instagram or even the best steps to take to see results. As some companies have found out, if you are not a celebrity, it takes a lot of extra work to get famous on Instagram.

While this may be true, most companies aren't really looking to get famous. Instead, they are looking for a way to get a solid presence on the platform, a presence that will allow them to connect and engage with their target market. Instagram is a great way to showcase all of your different products through pictures, and it is growing so much every day. Finding your voice in the crowd can sometimes be a challenge. But with the tips in this chapter, you can make it happen for you.

Add Hashtags into Your Strategy

While the image that you put up on your page is very important to the success of your Instagram campaign, hashtags are one of the most important elements of your post. Captions can tell a story with the image, but the hashtag will get your image seen by those who may not be your current followers. When users on Instagram start to search for hashtags that are relevant in a specific industry, you want to make sure that your posts are one of the ones that show up. If they don't, then this means your competitors are there instead, and you are missing out.

The three main strategies that can be used for choosing hashtags:

1. Use hashtags that are pretty popular, ones that have the best chance of getting searched for. This may end up with a lot of competition, but it still increases your chances of being seen.

2. Use some hashtags that are less popular, but still highly relevant to the work that you want to do. These may drive fewer users to your

posts, but the ones who find you based on these hashtags are going to be more targeted.

3. Use hashtags that are often thought to attract new followers. Some of the good ones to go with include #follow, #follow4follow, and #followme.

No matter which of the three strategies you choose to go with or even if you decide to do a little combination of each one, try to use at least one hashtag on each post. Even more hashtags can be better because it increases the amount of reach you can get on this site.

Join the Instagram Community

As you will find with all kinds of social networking, Instagram is going to work the best when you use it to form a good relationship with others. You shouldn't just go through and post pictures in your own little vacuum. It is all about participating in and forming a community around these pictures. It needs to benefit everyone, not just yourself.

There are a variety of methods that you can use to be a

part of the community found on Instagram. Using things like hashtags will allow you a way to connect with many users you may not have met otherwise. Liking and commenting on pictures of other people can help you to be more engaged with the greater community. Participating in Instagram campaigns intended to help out worthy causes can make it easier for you to contribute to the greater good. And, if you share videos and images from an event, it can help your followers feel like they were in on the action.

Know How Often to Post to Get Optimal Results

There is a lot of conflicting advice out there on how often you should post on Instagram. Ultimately, only you can decide what is going to work best for your audience. With that said, Union Metrics provides some ideas on how to test out your efforts to see what will work best when it comes to posting frequency for your business.

According to their research, which was based on monitoring 55 different brands on Instagram, Union Metrics found that most brands post about 1.5 times a day. What is more notable is that posting more often didn't result in a decreased amount of engagement.

In the past, we were told to not post on our pages too often. While you may not want to go crazy and post every hour, posting 3 or 4 times a day is not a bad thing. It isn't going to drive your customers away, and it is pretty easy to work on to make sure you are more visible. You may want to start out with just posting one time a day, and then increase the frequency slowly from there. When you notice that there is a point when engagement goes down, then you can scale back to get to your optimal level.

Have Your Images Work with Your Brand's Vibe

If you take a look on Instagram, you will notice that some of the most successful brands who pay a lot of attention to how their images are contributing to their brand identity. They have an overarching theme that comes with their images, and this theme is going to be related to the overall image of the company. This helps people to feel like they really know you when they come to your Instagram page, and they are more likely to stay around and learn more about you as time goes on.

Learn the Right Ways to Optimize the Entire Profile

It really doesn't take that long of a time for you to go through and properly optimize the profile that you are using on Instagram, but it can definitely make a big difference on how many people will actually click on your site. It can also make a difference in how they view your brand. Below are some of the tips that you can follow to help optimize your profile.

- Make sure that the description and the images on your profile go well with the vibe that you want to see in your company.

- Make sure there is always a link present that goes back to your website. You could even consider setting up a landing page that is specific for your visitors from Instagram or you can make changes to the link to help promote a current campaign or other content.

- Use the logo for the company somewhere in the profile. This lets your users know that this profile is the official one for your company.

- Consider adding at least one brand-specific hashtag to your profile. This makes it easier for your customers to know the profile belongs to you.

- If you are a local business or you have your own store, consider including your physical location into the profile as well.

- Make sure that if you have other social media profile that your images and any other content stay consistent throughout.

Understand That Growing Your Followers Can Be an Art and a Science

Without having a good solid base of followers, all of the efforts that you do on Instagram are likely to be pretty fruitless. The secret to doing this though is pretty simple: you just need to have lasting engagement because that naturally leads to followers.

In other words, as you continue to post relevant and engaging images, the follower base is going to grow organically as well.

With that being said, there are a few strategies that you can use that will help to speed this process up a little bit more. Below are some of the strategies that you may want to consider using.

1. Remember that quality pictures and posts are always going to beat out quantity. If you have already started your account, make sure that you go through and edit it until only the very best is left. No one wants to follow you if all you have is thousands of pointless images that have nothing to do with your business.

2. Always have a good and relevant caption with your pictures. Asking a question within that caption can be a good way for you to increase your engagement.

3. Be consistent. Always remember who you are posting for and remember why you are posting.

71

4. Use various tools like Piqura to see which images are leading you to the highest engagement, and then post more of them.

5. Engage on the photos where you interact most, and also on other profiles. As people start to see that you are interacting on a regular basis, they are going to start following you as well.

6. Make sure that if you are on Instagram, you should promote this account everywhere that you go. Promote it to other social media sites, on your physical marketing materials, and to your email subscribers.

Be a Follower (We Promise It's a Good Thing!)

Unless you go on Instagram and you are already a big name, then you won't be able to get away without following people back. And not only should you follow your own followers back, but you also need to be active in finding new users to follow. Here are several strategies that you can use to make sure you are following the right kinds of people:

1. Find some people you already know. While you are logged in to your profile, go to the profile page and click on the top right-hand corner of the screen. Then tap on the 'Find Friends' and see who is on your Facebook friends list, contacts list, and suggested users list.

2. Search for any companies or people you know by utilizing the search bar on Instagram.

3. Find people you may like to follow by using the Search and Explore feature of Instagram. You just need to click on the magnifying glass icon and then scroll down to see who is being recommended.

4. Follow influencers in the industry that you are in. Keyhole helps you to search for posts and users by hashtag, and then you can sort through the results based on how many likes they have on their posts.

5. Follow any users who are following the influencers of your industry.

6. Search for hashtags that are industry-related. This is a great way to make sure that you find targeted users in your niche.

7. You can also do a search on Google for any of the influential users in your industry. You can type in something simple like "social media" + Instagram to have this work.

Post a Lot of Engaging Videos and Photos

It is easy for you to get stuck on posting the same type of content over and over again on any social media platform that you are using. Posting product shots and selfies can be part of your repertoire, but you also need to mix things up on occasion and change up your strategy. Also, spend this time monitoring the formats that you use and seeing which ones get the most engagement. There are a ton of different post ideas that you can go with including:

- User-submitted photos
- Images and videos that are based on a holiday theme
- Day in the life shots to help show off your own personal side

- Short tutorials or demos of the product
- Simple image quotes using tools like Canva
- Sneak peeks of any new products that you have available
- Some behind the scenes photos of your employees or workspace

As you go through and try to decide what is the best for you to post, you should also consider the strategies that will help convince your followers to like and comment on them. This will ensure that you are getting the most out of your posts and can lead to more engagement with your customers.

How to Turn My Followers into Customers

Part of this chapter discussed the importance of getting followers. Followers on your profile mean that there are more eyes looking at your content and, hopefully, purchasing your products. But how do you make sure that the followers you have actually become customers, rather than just glancing at your pictures and your content on occasion? Some of the things that you can do to help turn your followers into customers include:

1. *Create some trust*: One of the biggest ways that you can turn your followers into customers is to build up trust with them. You will find that Instagram is a great way to share details about you and your business with others and doing so can help humanize your business, which then creates trust with your followers. When your followers trust you, they are more likely to look into your services and they may choose you over the competition.

2. *Stay top of mind*: As you get more followers, actively like and comment on their posts as well. You can also use hashtags and handles which are relevant to the photos that you share and the ones you already know that the followers will search and click. Doing this will let your followers know that you are there and keep you top of mind, especially when they need you most.

3. *Make your followers feel like they are special*: When you can make your customers feel special, you will find they are more likely to follow the content that you post and more

likely to work with you. To do this, give them an exclusive experience on this site, share secrets and details that aren't available on other sites, and more.

4. *Include links and calls to action*: As you share your information and posts on Instagram, make sure that each one includes a call to action and a link to your website. This makes it easier for the customer to know what you want them to do when they finish reading your post.

5. *Showcase some of the unique qualities of your business*: When you post on a consistent basis, share more about yourself and your business, and connect well with your audience, you will find that your followers are much more loyal to you. Make sure that when you work on your Instagram profile, you create one that your followers want to be a part of, and they are more likely to become your customers.

Instagram is a great social media platform to work on. You can utilize their great picture format in order to showcase your work and the products that you are selling. When you can make a good connection with your followers and potential customers and you can create content that they really enjoy and find valuable, you will be able to get all of the customers you need from your Instagram account.

Other Tips You Can Use to Increase Your Reach with Instagram

Instagram can easily become one of the greatest tools out there to help you reach your customers and grow your business. There are currently more than 500 million users who are on Instagram each day, and this provides you with a huge pool that you can utilize for your own needs. If you want to make sure that your marketing is as good and effective as possible with Instagram, you need to make sure that you can increase your following on a consistent basis and that you keep these people around. The more people who follow you on Instagram and learn about your brand, the more people you will reach every time that you post something online.

There are a lot of things that you can do to make sure that the efforts you put into your Instagram marketing are successful. Below are some of the best tips and tricks that you may want to include in this plan:

1. Make sure to utilize all of the free tools that Instagram offers. Instagram has an option for you to create a business profile, similar to what we see with a business profile on Facebook. You can utilize this profile type to use those call to actions to get your customer to contact you or visit a certain page. You can also access various analytics about your page. Looking through these helps you to see exactly how your users are interacting with the content that you put there. You can then use this to make any of the necessary adjustments to increase follower engagement.

2. Take the time to cross-promote your post. If you would like to make sure that you can easily add the right followers to Instagram, ones who already love your brand, then you need to post across all of the social media followers on Facebook, Twitter, and more. Invite some of the followers you already have

there to come onto your Instagram account. As long as you provide them some value with doing this, you shouldn't have an issue with this one.

3. Never overwhelm your audience. You want to post enough on the page that you can keep your brand relevant, but you don't want to send out a post every five minutes either. You may have to experiment a bit in order to figure out the magic posting number that seems to work the best with you. Start with one or two times a day, and then change up the times to see what works for you.

4. Interact with your followers. Interaction is so important when it comes to being on social media, no matter which social media account you choose to go with. You can reply to the comments on your page or even do something like "Tag three of your friends who would love this!". This response can really help you to grow because it shows your customers that you are actually interested in them.

5. Pick out a hashtag that can be a bit interactive. Another idea that you may want to work with is to create a hashtag that is interactive and can create some engagement right away. A good way to do this is to make your own hashtag, and then ask any customer who actually purchases this product to post a picture of themselves with that product, adding in that hashtag as well. This can make it easier for more people to see and hear about your business because these hashtags are going to be shared with their friends along the way.

6. Be creative when it comes to connecting with your audience. When you are creative with the images that you are using, you don't want to put up the same boring pictures day in and day out. You need to find ways to get the attention of your followers and find ways to get them to actually click on you, rather than on someone else.

When you first get started on Instagram, it may seem like you have no idea of what you are doing. But this is still a great way to reach your potential customers and can work better for your business than Facebook, Twitter, and even YouTube, as long as you can use it properly. Use the tips that we discuss in this guidebook and you will be able to rock your marketing campaign on Instagram in no time.

Chapter 6: Marketing Your Business with YouTube

As a business, you will find that visual content has never been more effective or more popular, and YouTube continues to dominate when it comes to a social network that focuses on visuals. With about 85% of online adults considering themselves regular users of YouTube, the opportunities for your business to make a high-quality video and get it in front of a large and captivated audience is bigger than ever.

Why Is YouTube so Important?

YouTube is a bit different compared to some of the other social media sites that we have talked about. While Facebook is about providing good content to your customers and Instagram is more about using pictures to tell your story, YouTube spends time using videos to help you share your message with the customers you are looking for the most.

Videos are on the rise, and it is seen as one of the biggest growing media on the market. Many people are looking towards videos to get the news they want, to learn more about products, and so much more. While the other social media platforms can be used to help you reach your customers and spread some good content, they don't have the same impact as what you can get when you use videos and other visuals to your market.

YouTube is one of the best platforms to use to help you to do this. There are millions of daily users of YouTube, and, sometimes, it may seem that it is hard to reach your audience with all of the videos out there. But, if you utilize some of the other tools that you have at your disposal, such as your email list and other social media sites, you can get more followers to your YouTube page, and it won't take long before you see your page views increase.

How Can I Grow with YouTube?

YouTube is a social media site that a lot of businesses tend to avoid. They may spend some time on Facebook or Twitter or even Instagram, but if they do any videos, they simply put one or two on their websites and link back to the other social media sites they have. They forget the power that can come behind working on YouTube to reach customers and the competitive advantage they can get from doing this.

YouTube actually can present you with a ton of ways to help you grow your business, no matter what kind of business or industry that you are in. Below are some of the biggest ways that YouTube will help you see some major growth in your business:

1. *Visual media gets more customers*: You will find that content, especially visual content, is going to make a big difference in the response that you get from your customers. Humans are visual creatures. When you can create engaging videos, you can appeal to the passive learning aspect of human behavior and can really appeal to your visual nature.

2. *Tutorials and testimonials*: The best company videos are the ones that can share information, and even resources, on how your services and

products can perform for the customer. These videos could also include some great testimonials from the current or previous customers. These video testimonials make these accounts more tangible and can have a big effect on the prospects you have.

3. *Working with a playlist*: These playlists make it easier to create a nice list of videos that your viewers can check out in a series. This can make it easier for related content to be organized together, can guide users through a series of tutorials that you have, and more.

4. *Feedback and comments*: YouTube will provide you with a commenting system that lets people post some feedback on your videos. This provides you with a tremendous opportunity to interact with your potential customers and can even alleviate any concerns or questions right off the bat.

5. *Video social network*: Even though YouTube is basically a website to put a lot of videos on, it is also seen as a social network site just like

the rest of them we have talked about. It gives the user the ability to interact and engage as they want to with your brand, and it is a good way for you to build up a following with some of the users who are already on it.

6. *YouTube ads*: You can also choose to work with some paid options for advertising in order to get the most out of your YouTube page. By leveraging the YouTube ads that you have, it is easier to budget the money that you need to get the right traction in the early stages or to make sure that you provide a boost needed to your more mature profile.

7. *Customization*: YouTube provides you with some options so that you can add customizations to your page or your channel. This is a good way for you to integrate your business branding in with your profile and your channel so customers can get even more familiar with you.

8. SEO: One nice thing about YouTube is that it is set up to work with Google. This means that

you can perform some SEO on your videos, and if you pick the right keywords and start ranking high enough, your videos will start showing up in Google searches.

These are just a few of the benefits that you can get when it comes to working on your own YouTube channel. This is definitely a social media platform that a lot of businesses miss out on because they don't even think about it to begin with. But if you can provide fresh content on a regular basis to your customers, you will find that it is easier than ever to really reach your customers in new and innovative ways.

How Do I Interact with Other People on My Channel?

One of the most important things that you can do when you want to work on YouTube is that you need to interact with others. It is never a good idea to make a video, then post it up for others to see without ever making any comments or interacting with others who come and view or comment on your video. You may get a few views here or there, but it will start looking pretty superficial if people get on your channel and there never is any interaction from you.

This doesn't mean that you have to spend all day long on your computer waiting for a comment to appear. But it means that you should check in on a regular basis and respond and interact. Even spending a few minutes each day can be enough to make this happen. Your customers will appreciate the time you take to comment or reply back or even to answer some of the questions that they may have.

The more interaction you can add into the channel, the better. If someone comments on one of your videos, then make sure that you comment back to them, at least as much as you can. Over time, you will hopefully have a ton of followers and views, and it can be hard to reply to everything, but do the best that you can.

Just like with the other social media platforms, you also need to search around and find other places to respond and comment on as well. You can look through other videos in your industry and leave comments as well. Make sure that these comments are well thought out and that they make sense for the video that you just watched. If you do this properly, you will find that it can really help your business to grow as more and more people will notice your comments or your advice and will head over to your videos as well.

All About the Videos

When it comes to using YouTube, it is all about the videos. You need to fill up your channel with videos that are high-quality, informative and full of value to the customer. Having a lot of videos that meet these criteria can help you to extend your reach. Having a lot of videos just for the sole purpose of having a ton of videos is going to turn your customers off.

There are a few things that you can remember about posting the type of videos that you post. First, you need to come up with a good posting schedule that you can stick with. Your customers will rely on a good posting schedule. If they know that you always upload a video on Thursday evening, then they know the exact time to come back and look for something new. This is a great way to build up anticipation, and as more and more people talk about the video, it will be nice to have that steady timeframe for them to check in at.

You can choose any posting time that works the best for you. Just make sure that it is something that you can stick with and remain consistent with. If you are worried about not being able to get the video done each week on time, consider creating a few videos at a time and then having them ready to go anytime that you might fall behind.

Another thing that you must always have with each and every video you post is high quality. There are millions of videos found on YouTube, and many of them are done by professionals. If you want your business to be taken seriously in this market, then you must make sure that your videos are of the highest quality possible.

What this means is that you shouldn't have a video that looks like a home video or like something an amateur can do. If you don't have the resources or the experience to do it yourself, consider hiring a professional videographer to do the work. They can work on each video and make sure that it looks professional, that the videos are consistent and look good together, and that you get them uploaded in a timely manner.

The information that is inside of the videos also needs to be informative and provide some kind of value to your customers. Just making a video because it is that time of the week isn't going to help your business to grow. You need to have videos that teach your customers something, that let them know something new or provide value in some other way.

If you can, try to make a video that can go viral. This is really hard to do because often it is a surprise which videos are going to become viral. But if you can come up with a video idea that is going to catch the attention of a bunch of people, that will get them to share it a bunch as well. Doing this can help you to reach a ton of new people, many of whom may have never even heard about your business before but could become loyal followers and customers once they see the video. Take a look on YouTube and other sources and see what videos have become viral hits, and then try to see how you can adapt that to work for your industry as well.

And finally, no matter what kind of video you choose to work with—there are a ton of options (look at the next chapter to see some ideas)—you must make sure that you always have a call to action at the end. When the customer is done watching the video, what is it that you are hoping they will do? Do you want them to check out your website? Do you want them to like your video or look at some of the other videos that you have? Do you want them to make a purchase? You have to decide what you would like the customer to do, and then provide this in the call to action at the end of your video.

Working on YouTube can be a great experience. Visual content is becoming a huge marketing tool, one that will change the way that many businesses reach their customers and make sales. Being able to reach your customers with high-quality and valuable videos can often set you apart from your competition. In the next few chapters, we will take a closer look at some of the ways that you can market your brand or your business on YouTube, using both organic and paid advertising to help you out.

Chapter 7: Organic YouTube Marketing

If you have been toying with the idea of marketing your business through YouTube but you aren't sure where you should start or what you need to do, then this chapter is the one that you really need to read. Every business can benefit from using YouTube to promote themselves, and staying up-to-date on how it works, creating videos that your customers will find valuable, and learning how to reach the right people can make a big difference in how well you can use YouTube to help your business grow. Some of the different marketing tips that we will look at for YouTube include:

- Ways to optimize the videos that you create for searches and clicks
- The best types of videos for you to create and then have your customers share
- Ways to promote your videos, as well as your channel as a whole
- Ways to use paid YouTube ads to get your reach to extend as far as possible

How to Optimize Your Video to Get the Most Searches and Clicks

If you want to be successful on YouTube, you must make sure that you optimize all of your videos to work well with both Google and YouTube. By using the right keywords in your title, tags, and description can make it easier for your customers to find you if they do a search on you.

To start with is the title. Google often recommends that you use your keyword first, and then the branding second; this is to make it more SEO-friendly. You could also use season and episode numbers if that is relevant, but make sure this is at the end. The title that you create for your video should paint a clear picture of what the viewer is going to see if they click on your videos. Ideally, you will keep the title to 50 characters or less. You can make it longer, but often a title that is longer than this is going to be hard to read through, and this actually decreases the chances of someone clicking on your page.

You can also work with tags. These are going to be the main keywords that you want to have related to your video. Many people believe that YouTube is going to put the most weight on the first couple tags that you list out, so make sure that you rank your keywords with the most important ones near the front. If you can, try to use all 120 characters, but don't just put random keywords down if they don't relate to your video.

Next, you need to work with your description. You always want to make sure that there is a call to action so that your viewers can take the next step. This can include something like getting them to watch another video or click on your link. Then, the first few sentences will be displayed in search results, so make sure it has your value proposition there, maybe with a few important keywords in it as well.

Also, make sure to add in some high-quality thumbnails to help the viewer. When viewers are scrolling through the search results for YouTube, you may find that the right thumbnail can influence whether they decide to click on your video or not. The optimal size for these images would be 1280 px x 720 px. You could have YouTube automatically generate a thumbnail for you, but it is always best for you to create and upload your   own thumbnail.

What Types of Videos Should I Create and Share?

Just because you can upload a ton of videos to YouTube, doesn't mean that you should upload anything and everything that you can find. You need to make sure that you are creating and sharing high-quality videos, ones that actually showcase the products that you want to sell and will provide value to your customers.

One of the biggest questions that business owners will ask when they are considering marketing on YouTube is what types of videos they should consider posting. The prospect of coming up with the best ideas for making engaging and entertaining videos that also help you to make more sales can be hard. There are a lot of different kinds of videos that you can choose to go with to market on YouTube including:

1. *Tutorials*: These videos show your viewer how they should perform a certain task.

2. *Product demos*: These demonstrate some of the common uses for your products.

3. *Testimonials from customers*: You can make videos where you interview customers who were satisfied in the past. You can also share a user-generated testimonial on your own channel.

4. *Intro video for your business*: YouTube will allow you to create what is known as a Chanel Trailer, where you can welcome all new viewers to your business. You can use this to provide a brief introduction to your business, letting the viewers know what kinds of videos they should expect to see if they decide to subscribe to this channel.

5. *Behind-the-scene videos*: You can even choose to take your viewers on a tour of your workspace or your office. If you have other employees, consider introducing the viewers to them.

6. *Tips and tricks*: If you have any, it is a good idea to provide some insights that will help your viewers and your prospects.

98

7. *Live presentations*: Any time that you can go live, you are providing a great service to your customers and really getting them interested. If you ever go and speak at a tradeshow or a conference, make sure to record and share this on your YouTube page.

8. *Webinars*: Most webinar software providers make it easy for you to record your webinars. You can then upload these to your YouTube channel and share with your audience.

9. *Commercials*: You can easily put your commercials on YouTube as well. If you need some ideas for the types of ads that work well on YouTube, check out Always and Old Spice.

10. *Product launches*: If you have a new product coming out to the market soon, share the release of this with some of your YouTube users so they know the news.

As you go through and create and promote different video types, it won't take long to learn the type that your audience seems to respond the best too. This will help you to target your advertisements to the audience you want to reach and can help you to make the content that works the best for your business.

How to Promote Your Videos as Well as Your YouTube Channel

The next thing we need to look at when it comes to organically reach with your videos is the different methods of how you can promote your videos and your channels. There are three main ways to get more views for the videos that you are creating and adding to your channel which include:

1. Getting a higher rank for YouTube or Google keyword searches
2. Having a large subscriber base on YouTube
3. Promoting your channel and your videos through other web properties

The previous section already took some time to discuss the best ways to optimize the videos that you are working on. Growing your channel on YouTube and being able to promote these channels and videos on other web properties that you own will be the next, and, sometimes, it is the most challenging part of this whole process. Some of the ways that you can help increase your views and subscribers to your videos include:

1. *Promote these videos and your YouTube channel on the other social media profiles*: You should include some hashtags that are relevant to these posts so that you get even more reach.

2. *Engage with your loyal fans*: When you spend time looking through the Creator Dashboard, you will see which users are the most engaged with the content you provide. You can consider involving these fans in some way to nurture some brand ambassador relationships later on.

3. *Add a widget for YouTube on your blog*: You can use a tool such as Tint to help you display a number of videos—can be your own or someone else's—in a widget that goes right on your blog or website.

4. *Collaborate with other business owners who run a complimentary niche*: Approach some other YouTubers and see if they are willing to promote your videos if you promote theirs. You can even consider co-branding videos to use them for both audiences.

5. *Engage with your users, both on their videos and on yours*: Social media sees the best results when you interact and engage with others users, but this doesn't mean that you should just stay on your own channel. Leave comments that are thought out well on videos and respond to any comments left on yours. Remember, the more interactions you have with your videos, the higher you will rank in the search.

6. *Share your videos on your email list*: Direct the audience to your embedded videos on your site to increase your page views and your video views.

7. *Embed the videos onto your blog or website*: Add videos to existing posts on your blog or you can even come up with new blog posts that are specifically there to promote your videos. This will help you to increase your video views and increase your page views on the site.

Making your reach organic on YouTube can take some time and may not happen as quickly as you would like. But, it is a great way to ensure that you are finding people who are truly interested in the content that you try to provide. There are also some paid options that you can choose to work with as well, but whether these are going to be as successful as the organic reach that we have just talked about, it depends on your audience, on the products that you are trying to sell, and more.

Chapter 8: Paid YouTube Marketing

Just like with some of the other social networks that we have talked about, there are ways to use YouTube and extend the reach of your content in a manner that is much faster than organic reach. YouTube ads will allow you to turn any of the videos that you have into an ad for your business. When you do this, it makes sure that your video is going to be seen before other videos when a potential viewer types in keywords related to your business. This can also be used to have your video show up alongside other videos that YouTube users are watching at the time, if they relate to the topics in your video.

There are several different targeting options that you can use when you set up YouTube ads. You can target based on things like location, gender, age, keywords, and more. You can also choose the size of your ad. Some people will choose to go with a large masthead that is somewhere between 850 by 250 or the smaller standard display ads that are either 300 by 250 or 300 by 600.

Using YouTube ads can be a good way for you to make sure that the videos you produce get a nice boost. For someone who is just getting started on YouTube, these ads can help you to get off the ground and can increase your social proof, which can include things like comments, views, and thumbs up.

There are many different options that you can choose to work within YouTube marketing when it comes to paid advertising, but the YouTube ads are usually the most commonly used one. If you are going to pick a video to advertise, make sure that you pick a high-quality video, one that has the potential to go viral and one that is likely to get people back to your channel to watch more videos or to make a purchase.

You have to be careful when you choose to work with YouTube ads. While it can provide you with a ton of benefits for your business and can bring more viewers and potential customers back to your page, you have to make sure that you are picking out good videos, and that you are providing value to your customers.

105

Here are some of the best practices that you must keep in mind as a business owner who wants to use YouTube ads to increase their reach:

1. Make sure that when you create or pick out a video for this, the first few seconds act as a hook. This hook is what you need to real the viewers in to watch the rest of the video. If you cannot capture the attention of the viewer in the first 5 seconds, then they are not going to stick around. Figure out what is your most captivating content first, and then back this up with the details and facts later in the video.

2. Keep the ads short and sweet. Most experts on YouTube recommend that if you are going to make a video ad, keep it to one minute or less. Unbounce found that about 80% of your viewers are going to click out of the ad after a minute anyway, making it too long is just going to be a waste of your time. Shorter video ads are very important when using this service.

3. Focus on the goals of the advertisement, rather than on the views. While it is important to have some on-site engagement, and this can be a great indicator that the video is hitting the marks that you want with your viewers, take a look at whether or not your YouTube ads are helping you meet your specific goals. Are these views resulting in more conversions or even sending the right kind of traffic to your site? If the answer is no, then it is time to make some adjustments.

4. Make sure there is a call to action in your video. We have mentioned this a bit before, but it is important to always have a call to action present in every video, especially in your advertisements. This helps to increase the amount of engagement that you are getting from your customers. If you are working with the TrueView ads (we will bring these up in a bit), you can choose if you would like to overlay the call to action over the ad, ensuring that viewers are going to see this call to action right when they see the video start.

5. Before you record the video for the ad, always have a goal in mind. What are you hoping to get people to do when they are done watching the ad? Do you want them to visit your website? Do you want them to follow your channel? Do you want them to call your business? Do you want them to purchase something? Having this specific goal in mind ahead of time will make it easier to monitor the effectiveness of these ads.

6. Consider video remarketing to get more engagement: Remarketing, which is sometimes called retargeting, will allow you a chance to target these ads to users who interacted with your YouTube channel or videos in the past. This makes it easier for you to achieve a positive return on investment for any ads that you want to make on YouTube.

As you spend your investment on a marketing strategy for YouTube, remember to focus on the content and what you put into your video before you even think about starting a marketing campaign to go with it. With more than 300 hours of video being added to

YouTube each minute, you know that the playing field on this site is crowded and you must make sure that all of your videos can speak to your audience and provide them with value for it to succeed. Then, once you have had the time to create a video that meets all of these criteria, you will be able to promote and distribute it through all of the channels that you have, and then add in some paid promotion as well.

Working with TrueView

One thing to consider when you are ready to do paid advertising with YouTube, you will hear about TrueView InStream ads. These are basically the way that YouTube is going to create commercials similar to what you may see when watching your favorite shows on live television. This is one of the most successful forms of online advertising that YouTube can offer to businesses.

When you decide to take out a TrueView ad, you are going to create a short video for your channel or brand, one that can encourage potential customers to learn more about your company. These are the ads that will show up at the beginning of a monetized video, but if there are some videos that are longer in length, these ads can show up in the middle of them as well.

However, if there is a video on YouTube that is non-monetized, there will never be ads that show up on it. If you would like to see your commercial show up on a specific channel, make sure that you check and see if that channel is monetized before you go any further. If it is, you can set up the ad to be shown on those videos. If it isn't, then you will have to do something else.

Another way that you can work with TrueView is with their InDisplay ads. These are going to show up as a thumbnail next to a video that someone is watching at that time. These will sometimes look like the PPC ads you see from other sources, but they have a thumbnail next to them. People will then be able to choose when and if they click on your ads. These ads are sometimes used to promote other videos that you created and put on your channel. These InDisplay ads can also be a good way for you to jump start or even restart a viral campaign.

There are a lot of different options that you can utilize when it comes to TrueView, and you can be a bit creative to stand out from the crowd. You will notice though that when you use some of these TrueView ads, you are not going to be billed in the same manner that you are for a regular AdWords ad that you would place with Google.

InStream ads are going to be billed on a cost per view format. This means that you will be charged any time someone clicks on your ad and then stays there for a minimum of 30 seconds. If this happens, regardless of the conversion or not, you will have to pay. If the viewer doesn't click on the ad or they don't stay for the 30 seconds, then you won't have to pay for that.

Keep in mind that a lot of YouTube ads are going to allow your potential viewer to skip the ad after only 3 seconds has passed if they are using either a desktop or mobile device. This could be good news for you. If someone happens to see your brand for 3 seconds or even slightly longer then skips the commercial, they could potentially head to your YouTube channel later on to learn some more about you. If they make a purchase and more, then you got a potential customer without having to pay for them.

The InDisplay ads that we talked about before are going to be a cost per view format as well. You will be charged any time that a potential customer clicks on your video's thumbnail and starts to watch the video on their watch page. If the customer sees your ad and doesn't click on it, then you won't be charged for that view. But if the customer clicks on it and watches it even for a short amount of time, then you will be charged for that customer.

These are the two main options that you can use when you want to do paid advertising on YouTube. The way that you become more effective with YouTube marketing is to create a good video, one that sets you apart from the competition and all of the other videos that are found on YouTube. This may mean that you need to focus more on the video that you are creating so that you can really entice the customer and to ensure that your YouTube paid promotions are as effective as possible.

A Few Words About Remarketing Your YouTube Viewers

One neat thing that you can do is show a personalized ad to millions of viewers all across YouTube and other partner sites based on how they interacted with your channel or your videos in the past. This is known as a process of video remarketing. By reinforcing your message to those who have already gone through and seen your channel or your videos, you will find even more success with a better return on investment since these viewers showed interested in your products or videos in the past.

There are a lot of great benefits that can come from using YouTube remarketing. Some of these benefits include:

- *A better return on investment*: Advertisers who use remarketing on YouTube have been able to improve their return on investment. This is because they are showing these videos to people who already showed some interest in the product or the service.

- *Broader scope*: With the big YouTube network, it is possible that your video ad will reach a lot of potential customers, all of whom are on the remarketing list.

- *Efficient pricing*: The Google Ads auction model that you will use for these is going to provide you with some competitive rates to help meet the return on investment that you want. With the CPV bidding, you are going to pay for views on the video and some other types of interactions with the video, such as the call to action overlays, clicks on the video, cards, and companion banners.

- *Flexibility*: You will find that website remarketing, which can also be known as retargeting or remessaging, will be based on the actions of the visitor on your website. You can go through and remarket based on the actions that are specific to your YouTube videos, including things like when viewers like, dislike, comment on, and share your video.

So, how does this whole process work? Remarketing lists can be created when you take the time to link together your Google Ads and your YouTube channel account. Once you have a chance to link these accounts, you can create your own remarketing lists, ones that will reach the customers and people who have done the following YouTube related actions:

- Shared a video from your channel
- Commented on a video from your channel
- Added any video from your channel to a playlist
- Linked any video from your channel
- Visited a channel page
- Took the time to subscribe to your channel
- Viewed certain videos as an ad
- Viewed any video as an ad from a channel
- Viewed certain videos
- Viewed any video from a channel

You can then use these lists when you are looking through the settings for targeting for new or existing campaigns. You can always go through and manage your lists any time that you need, simply by selecting the Shared library and then Audiences if you are using the previous ads experience or the Audience manager if you are now using the new Google Ads experience. One thing to note here is that you cannot make these remarketing lists from any of the views you get on your bumper ads.

There are several best practices that you can try to use when it comes to doing a remarketing campaign. You are already marketing to people who have shown some interest in your business or your products, so that is a good start in the beginning. But you also want to make sure that you get the best return on investment with your remarketing lists. Below are some of the features that you should explore in order to make this happen:

- *Try out different formats for your ad*: You can build and then target the remarketing campaign that you are doing with various video ads along with other creative formats that are available, including rich media ads, images, and text.

116

- *Engage with your mobile customers*: Mobile advertising is growing like crazy and more and more of your potential customers will find you through their mobile devices. You can work with square and vertical videos to make it easier to engage with these customers when they find you on the YouTube app.

- *Detailed reports*: You can optimize your remarketing campaign based on performance metrics. You could choose to raise bids on certain channels or specific topics, for example, which help you generate the best response to your ads.

- *Ease of use*: You should make sure that you are creating, managing, and targeting these remarketing lists as best as possible.

- C*ustom audiences*: You even get the option of customizing your targeting by combining your remarketing lists together and seeing what happen. For example, you could reach audiences who viewed your movie trailer, but maybe hadn't seen the ad that promoted the release of the DVD.

Remarketing is just one of the ways that you can market your business on YouTube. It is often seen as one of the most effective methods though because it allows you to reach your customers, especially those who already viewed your content in the past. These customers are more likely to be interested in your business or in your product compared to others, and targeting them in these campaigns can really make a difference in the conversions you get.

Chapter 9: Using Twitter to Grow Your Business

The next social media site that we are going to look at is Twitter. With more than 313 million active users each month and a demographic that is young too, Twitter can be a great place for you to market yourself and see some great results. And you will find that it is pretty easy to set up your own Twitter profit. You just need to come up with your own handle (the name of your profile), upload a good picture to be your profile picture, fill out a bio, and send out the first tweet, and you are ready to go. There are more steps to growing the account, but these simple steps will at least help you to get yourself started.

Growing a real following through Twitter can take some more work than just sending out tweets when you have a big event or a new product. Twitter is useful because it helps you to engage with your audience and actually interact with them. This isn't going to happen if you just send out a few tweets a year. Let's take a closer look at Twitter and how it can help you grow your business.

119

How Is Twitter Different from the Rest?

The approach that you have to each social media site that you work with should be a bit different. You won't be able to use the same strategy that you do with Twitter as you do with your Facebook marketing plan. It is important that you learn more about the way Twitter works and the best way to use it to get the best benefits.

There are many different ways that a business can utilize Twitter to reach their needs. Some of the main ways include:

- Managing their reputation
- Branding themselves
- Networking so they can find other similar businesses and potential customers in the industry
- Interacting with their customers and potential customers
- Driving engagement for some of the promotional activities that they are working on
- Sharing the content and information that they have about their business and about their products

Just like with all of the other social media sites that we have talked about, most of these activities have something to do with interactions. It is not just about broadcasting out your content, like what can happen with Pinterest and Instagram sometimes. Twitter works because of open communication.

Now that we know a bit about the importance of Twitter and how businesses will often use it, it is time to go into some of the things that you need to know in order to get started with marketing on Twitter. We will go beyond the how to for setting up a good profile. We will look at some of the real strategies that will ensure you can reach your customers and that you won't waste your time through this platform.

Finding Your Untapped Market Through Twitter Chats

Many marketers have started to ask how they can get more followers on Twitter. But the real question that should be done here is how do you get more active Twitter followers? As any business knows, just because you have a bunch of followers doesn't mean that they are interacting with you or even seeing the things that you are posting. If you have 100 followers but only 5 of them are active and seeing your posts, that isn't such a good thing.

The answer to this problem is Twitter chats. These chats have been pushed for a bit of time, but many marketers have been slow to try them out and see what power they can get out of them. But as more people try them, the popularity is growing. Getting into these chats now could be a great way for you to see some results with finding not just followers, but active followers on Twitter.

The reason that this tool is so effective is that people who use them are the ones who already are active on Twitter. You aren't going to find inactive users on the platform. They won't just use it to distribute or consume content. Instead, these people are on Twitter and using it for the purpose it was designed for, which is to interact. These followers are great because they are the ones who will reply to the Tweet you put up, they will retweet your content, and they can help you spread your message.

When you are ready to start on Twitter chats, make

sure you look for some that are in your related industry. There are a lot of Twitter chat groups so make sure to find one that will work for your needs and your industry. But if you find there aren't any options for you, then you can start out your own. Either way, the key to seeing some success with Twitter chats is to ensure that you are more than a spectator. You must be there, interacting and adding value along with others, or this trick won't work for you at all.

Always Plan Ahead

Never wait until a big event or even a big holiday before you start planning out some of your posts. For example, by late September or early October, you should already have your tweets and content ready to go live for Halloween. When November comes, you should have some tweets ready for Thanksgiving and then on to Christmas.

Taking the time to plan ahead of the holidays and any other special events that occur in your company can ensure that you have plenty of time. You can use this to pick out trending hashtags for your topics and create some high-quality content without feeling rushed.

Instead of waiting until a few days before, you should make it your goal to come up with a campaign not later than 2 weeks before the scheduled time. There are also various calendars that you can find online that will help you look at the upcoming holidays so you can make a comprehensive plan of what you want to write your tweet for.

Once that special day comes up, whether it is Halloween, Christmas, Thanksgiving, or some other day, you can then follow any of the trending hashtags for that event. You can also choose to send out content as events are happening, rather than waiting until the momentum is done to get it up and working. This is one of the benefits of working with Twitter.

Make Sure That Your Tweets Are Always Conversational

Remember that Twitter is similar to your other social media sites in that you need to interact and have a conversation with the people you are talking to on the site. Often, this is something forgotten, and then they wonder why they aren't seeing the results that they were looking for when they got started on this social media site.

The way that many different companies look at Twitter and the way they decide to tweet is going to be very one dimensional. These companies will write out tweets that are just broadcasts, which is not really what Twitter should be about. Your Tweets are not headlines with a link like a newspaper. They shouldn't just be funny statements or inspirational quotes either. Instead, they need to be able to open up the door for a lot of conversation and communication between you and your customers.

The good news is that you don't have to just use your personal account to engage with their customers. It is easy for a business to benefit from this kind of personalization in the communication that they provide to their customers. Some of the tips that you can use to make this all happen includes:

1. Make some of your tweets questions to your followers, rather than just posting news all of the time.

2. Try to get about 30-40% of your tweets into replies to other people.

3. When you want to add a link into your tweet, add in at least a line of your own insight. This helps to spark the conversation a bit more and will make it more likely that others will respond to your tweet.

4. You should try to tweet directly to the audience. Instead of writing out something like "Blog Post Title" and then a link, you could ask a question like "What do you all think of this new post?" to help get others to interact a bit more.

Taking the time and effort to be a bit more conversational on your tweets can mean a higher amount of engagement. And over the long term, this is going to result in more activity for your Twitter account as a whole. And when you are more active and more responsive, it could result in a lot of new customers, and that can   help your bottom line.

Create a Good Tweeting Strategy and Schedule

This one is similar to planning ahead, but it can be used all throughout the year, rather than just at big events. For this one, you should have a set posting schedule that works for your Twitter account. This tweeting schedule should take the time to detail when and what you plan to tweet on your page. The number of times that you decide to tweet will vary based on your goals and what seems to work the best for your business. Some people will do a tweet once a day, while others may find that doing it 3 times seems to work the best for them and their customers.

This strategy can list out the times you are going to post, and you can even write out the posts that you want to have show up on the profile ahead of time. This strategy can also take some time to outline things like when you are going to link something in a tweet, when you are going to release a new product, when you are going to share information, and more.

You should include all of this as a part of an overall content strategy. This is important if you publish your content through many platforms such as Twitter, Facebook, and a blog. This strategy is going to be so important and ensures that people see the things that you want them to.

For example, you must ensure that your customers are seeing the link to your blog or your product more than one time. There is a chance that they will miss out on it the first time or maybe forgot about it. If you just post the link one time, then you are missing out on a lot of potential customers. With your Twitter planning strategy, you can make sure that you get the post link listed more than once so that you have a better chance of reaching your potential customers and you don't end up not posting more than once.

Twitter Video

While Twitter is not always the first option that people will think about when they want to get started with video marketing, this is still something that you can consider adding into your Twitter marketing campaign. Twitter may not be as advanced with video marketing as you will see with YouTube, but it gives you a few options that can be helpful when you want to promote using videos on this site.

The first option is to use the native video feature that is already available through Twitter. This feature is going to allow you to record videos that are up to 140 seconds long. When these videos are done, you can upload these straight to the stream on your Twitter profile. If you want to make things easier and your videos is going to be about 2 minutes or less, then this option can be a great one to choose. If you would like to do something a bit longer or you would like some more features to use, then you may want to go with the second option.

Another option that you can go with when you use Twitter is Periscope. This is a live streaming app that Twitter actually owns. Periscope can integrate your content into Twitter, which means that if you do a live stream, this is going to show up on the Twitter feeds for your followers. Then, when the stream is over, that recording will still sit around so your viewers can watch it whenever is the most convenient for them.

The second option can be nice because you get the chance of going live. This attracts more attention from your potential customers because they can watch you, ask you questions, and so much more. Add in the fact that these live videos were able to get more than 31 million views in 2016, and more as time has gone on, it is definitely worth your time to add at least a few of these videos onto your Twitter feed on occasion.

Set Some Goals and Some Milestones

No type of marketing campaign is going to be complete if you don't have some measurable goals that you would like to see done at a certain point. Without these goals, objectives, and milestones, you may as well quit now. This is because you are setting yourself up to make the same mistakes that other companies are going to fall into when they decide it is time to work on their own social media marketing, whether it is with Twitter or other sites.

In fact, at least 41% of companies state that they really don't know if their efforts in social media are working or not. This is never a good thing because it means that these many companies are wasting money without knowing if they are being successful or not. A big reason that many companies feel this way is that they aren't really keeping good track of their activities, and they aren't setting the right objectives that are needed to see success.

What most businesses do instead is just publish some content on one of their social media accounts, and then they just publish some content in the hopes that it will do something to help the brand without having any plan to go with it, and then praying it will not work well with Twitter. The first option here is to set up the goals and the objectives that you want to see when you are on Twitter. Some of the different objectives that you may want to consider for your business include:

- Build up a following that is engaged
- Monitor and then find ways to improve the reputation of your brand
- Network with other bloggers, as well as the influencers, who are found in your industry
- Try to drive some more traffic over to your website
- Find ways to get   more leads

- Respond to any of the complaints that you get from the customer as quickly as possible

You have to choose the objectives that seem to work best for your needs. You won't be able to work on all of these at once. But picking out one at a time to improve can make a big difference. Once you have your objective picked out, you will then need to establish some accomplishments that will be able to tie in with those objectives. Some of the things that may work for this and can help you measure how well your objective is being followed and accomplished includes the following:

1. Add in a minimum of 100 new contacts to your Twitter page.
2. Improve the referrals that you get out of Twitter by at least 30 percent.
3. Generate a minimum of 20 leads from the posts that you do on Twitter.
4. Make sure that your response time is under 10 minutes (or another time frame that works for your business).
5. Keep the response rate to your customers over 90%. This means that you are going to interact

with customers, as many as possible, so they know you are there and paying attention.

6. Increase the amount of retweets and @mentions by 15 percent.

And before we finish here, make sure that all of the goals you set have a very specific deadline. You could set it for a week, a month, a quarter, or whatever tends to work the best for you. This helps you to determine if the strategy is working well for you, and if you need to make any adjustments.

Paid Advertising on Twitter

Just like with the other social media sites, you have the option of doing paid advertising with Twitter. Twitter ads are great for helping you get a good message out in front of the users, the ones who are the most likely to show some interest in your brand and in your products. According to data provided by Twitter, ad engagement has increased by 69%, while the cost per ad engagement has dropped by 28%. Add in that there are new ad formats that you can choose from with Twitter, and it is the perfect time for you to try running a Twitter ad for yourself.

There are a lot of different options that you can choose from when it comes to Twitter ads. Some of the best options that you can choose from include:

1. **Promoted Tweets**

    These types of tweets are simply tweets that you are going to pay to get displayed to people on Twitter who are not following you yet. They can work just like regular tweets in that others can comment on them, like them, and even retweet them as they like. They will also look like regular tweets in many cases, other than they will have a Promoted label on them.

    These tweets are going to appear on the users' timeline or on their profile, near the top of search results, and even on the desktop and mobile apps for Twitter. This is a great way to discuss your brand and let new potential followers know more about you. If you are careful with the way that you set these up and you make them really informative and valuable, it is likely that you will get a ton of interactions. The more interactions, the more people who will see the advertisement and the easier it will be for you to get new followers.

2. *Promoted Accounts*

Another option that you can work with is a promoted account. These are sometimes known as Followers campaign. They will make it easier for you to promote the account you are using for business to targeted users who aren't following you yet, but who may find some of your content interesting. This can be a great way to find people who are already interested in topics in your industry, so they are more likely to start following you.

These accounts will show up on the timelines of those people you follow. They can also show up in the Who to Follow suggestions and search results. They will list out that they have been promoted, but they will also have a Follow button on them, so your potential customers have a chance to click and start following your page.

3. *Promoted Trends*

When you see that a topic is trending on Twitter, it means that it is one of the most talked about subjects. It also is a topic that is going to appear on the timeline of different users, on their Explore tab, and on the Twitter app. If you do a promoted trend, you will be able to promote a hashtag of your choice at the top of this list so it gains a lot more visibility.

When a user decides to click on this promoted trend, they are going to see an organic list of search results on that topic. What is different here though is that Promoted Tweet from your business will be the very first option at the top of this list. As people start to pick up on this specific hashtag and they decide to use it for their own tweets, you will start to gain more organic exposure which will increase the reach that you are able to get for your campaign.

One thing to keep in mind when you want to do a promoted trend is that these are not going to be available for any business or advertisers who are doing the self-serve options on Twitter.

4. *Automated Ads*

If you are pretty new to the whole idea of advertising on social media and you are a little unsure about what you should do or even how much you can spend or your marketing team is small and doesn't have a lot of available time, then working with Twitter Promote Mode may be the best option for you.

If you choose to go with Twitter Promote Mode, it is going to cost you about $99 USD each month. When you turn it on, the first ten tweets that you do for that day will automatically be promoted over to the audience that you have selected, as long as this selected audience passes the quality filter from Twitter. Replies, quote tweets, and retweets are never going to be promoted. You will also get a Promoted Account campaign that is ongoing.

You need to go through a bit and make some adjustments and add in the different specifications that you want. For example, you have to write out the tweets that you want to use, the audience that you would like to target, and more. According to estimates that Twitter gives, accounts that work with Twitter Promote Mode can reach about 30,000 additional people and gain an average of 30 new followers each month.

As you can see, there are a number of different benefits that come with working on Twitter. Twitter is a great way for you to promote your business and open up communication with your customers in a way that just isn't found with other sites. Rather than just posting information (although you can do this on occasion), you will spend time in conversations with your customers, interacting with them, and more. Twitter can be a great idea to implement into your marketing campaign to get the most out of reaching your customers.

Conclusion

Thanks for making it through to the end of *Social Media Marketing Secrets*. Let's hope it was informative and able to provide you with all of the tools you need to achieve your goals whatever they may be.

The next step is to use the information that we discussed in this guidebook to create your own social media marketing plan. There are so many benefits that come with having a presence on at least a few different social media sites. These sites are where a ton of your customers are right now, and not taking advantage of them simply means you are letting your competition beat you. This guidebook tells you all of the secrets and tips that you need to get started with your own social media marketing campaign.

In this guidebook, we had taken some time to talk about the top names in social media, namely Facebook, Instagram, YouTube, and Twitter. All of these can help you to reach your customers and see great results, as long as you are willing to put in the work and as long as you understand how each platform works. This guidebook spent time looking at each one in more depth and explored some of the marketing strategies that you can use to make each one work. There are also other social media sites that you may have interest in and figuring out the one that meets with your audience and where they like to spend time, and you can use some of the same tips to help you out there.

Social media should be a part of any business's marketing plan. There are so many customers who spend a good amount of time on social media, and this is a great way to build trust and interact with your customers to turn them into purchasers. Make sure to read through this guidebook and learn more about the best social media marketing tips.

Instagram 2019 Marketing

Secrets To Growth Your Brand, Be an Influencer of Millions and Advertising your Business with this Guide on Social Media Marketing

Jack Gary

The information in the following pages is broadly considered a truthful and accurate account of facts and as such, any inattention, use, or misuse of the information in question by the reader will render any resulting actions solely under their purview. There are no scenarios in which the publisher or the original author of this work can be in any fashion deemed liable for any hardship or damages that may befall them after undertaking information described herein.

Additionally, the information in the following pages is intended only for informational purposes and should thus be thought of as universal. As befitting its nature, it is presented without assurance regarding its prolonged validity or interim quality. Trademarks that are mentioned are done without written consent and can in no way be considered an endorsement from the trademark holder.

Table of Contents

Introduction

The following chapters will discuss everything you need to know in order to use Instagram for your business. There are a lot of different parts that come together when it comes to creating a high-quality marketing plan. You want to make sure that you are reaching your customers where they are located and make sure that you do things that your competition is missing out on. Instagram is one place where you can do both effectively.

In this guidebook, we will explore all of the different parts that you need to consider when it comes to creating a following and marketing on Instagram. This platform is a bit different compared to some of the other social media sites you may have heard about or used in the past. It focuses more on interacting and creating some great videos and pictures for your customers to take a look at. Yes, you can add captions and more, but the majority of it is focused on images and being more visual.

This guidebook will get into depth about the benefits

of using Instagram, how to set up your business account, and some of the best steps to take to utilize the Instagram Stories feature. We will also look at the different ways that you can gain more followers to your account, the importance of interacting with your followers and other pages to gain more followers, and some tips to make you as efficient as possible with your posts.

To finish off this guidebook, we will look at how you can gain more attention and followers through paid advertising, how to get the most out of your marketing through Instagram, some of the different ways that you can make money on Instagram, and success stories of other marketers who used Instagram to grow their business.

There is just so much you can do when it comes to growing your business through Instagram, and it is definitely a tool that small businesses, individual promoters, and larger companies can benefit from. When you are ready to learn more about Instagram and what you can do with it to grow your own business, make sure to read through this guidebook to get started.

Chapter 1: The Basics of Instagram and Why You Should Use It

There are many different social media sites that you can choose to work with when it is time to grow your business. Individuals, marketers, and many businesses have found that social media is one of the best ways to reach their customers and build up trust in a way that just isn't possible with the other forms of marketing that are out there. These sites allow you to talk with your customer, form a relationship, show your products, and so much more.

While there are many choices when it comes to social media, one option that your business should consider if they want to really reach their customers and even gain an edge over the competition is Instagram. Instagram is a bit different from some of the other social media sites such as Twitter and Facebook. This site focuses on pictures and visuals that can really get your customers interested in your products. There are also features to make

149

short videos that can do well on Instagram.

No matter what you are marketing or trying to sell on Instagram, you will find that there is a big audience that is there, waiting to hear more from you. If you are able to provide high-quality pictures, show that you care about your customers by interacting with them, and can be consistent with your posting, you will find that Instagram may be exactly what you are looking for to help grow your own business.

There are a lot of different reasons why you should consider going with Instagram, either instead of or in addition to Twitter, Facebook, and other social media sites. Some of the biggest reasons why you should add Instagram to your marketing campaign include:

More engagement from users

Depending on the quality of your post, some of the updates that you do on Twitter and Facebook will be ignored by the user. This isn't quite the same when it comes to users of Instagram. When you have an Instagram account that is active and you fill it up with content that is interesting and valuable to your customer, you will be able to increase the engagement you have with your audience to crazy levels. In fact, a study that was just done by Forrester found that posting on Instagram could result in 58 times more engagement per each follower you have compared to Facebook, and 120 times more than you get on Twitter.

Whether you are a business trying to grow your reach or an individual who is looking for ways to earn money on Instagram, this engagement is key. It means that people are actually looking at the content that you post. It means they are liking it, commenting on it, and leaving you questions and advice. This makes it easier for you to sell products to them and can increase the amount of money that you can make on this site.

Lots of potential customers

No matter what industry you are in, you will find there are a ton of customers just waiting to meet you and hear about your products. In fact, there are more than 150 million users on Instagram, making it the best and most used platform for sharing photos and this number is growing every day. This allows you to share photos and some shorter videos with your followers any time that you want. And since the number of businesses who use this platform is still pretty low, it is easy to find your customers and beat out the competition when you are on this platform.

Building up your personality and trust with the customer

With branded content helping you to gain more engagement, one of the best things about working with Instagram is that it helps you to build up trust. Your customers are never going to purchase anything from you if they don't have trust in you, and without a good emotional connection, you are going to lose business to the competition.

With Instagram, you can build up this trust and this emotional connection, which can then help you to reach more customers overall. Instagram makes it easy for you to share the experiences that occur each day with your business, in a manner that is casual and informal, which can give a more personal feel to the business. This is something that a lot of your customers are going to like and can help you to grow by leaps and bounds.

There are a lot of ways that you can make your business feel more personal. You can showcase some photos of behind the scenes of your business, or even employee images because these tend to work well on Instagram. This helps to show off some of the people who work with you and seems to rank a lot of service industries higher on the list of popular pages.

Increase your traffic

The more traffic you get to your profile and your website, the more potential profits you can make. There are a lot of companies out there and you have a ton of competition to fight against. Being able to increase your traffic and getting your business in front of others more often can make a big difference in the success that you see.

Although you aren't able to go through and add in a link for your customer to click on with every update you do on Instagram, you will still find that this social media site is a powerful source of traffic. Plus, when you add in higher levels of engagement compared to what you can get on Twitter and Facebook, you will find that creating and maintaining a profile that is strong on this site can be so important when it comes to making your website more visible.

Get an edge over the competition

Despite the popularity of Instagram and how it is growing so quickly, there is still a lot less competition for this site compared to Twitter or Facebook. According to a survey that was conducted by American Express, only about 2 percent of small businesses are on and using Instagram. This means that the ones that do go on this site are gaining a huge advantage over any competition in the industry. This is the perfect time to get in. You can make your voice heard in ways that you just can't with the other social media sites. Facebook and Twitter have been around for a long time, so the competition has had plenty of opportunities to get in there and make some noise.

But since many small businesses are not embracing Instagram (at least yet!), this means that you have an incredible opportunity to step up and cater to your customers right where they are. Before the competition catches up to you, you should consider getting started with

Instagram and start building up your following now.
You will also find that the businesses that take the time to incorporate this social media site into their strategy are the ones that have a much better time reaching the right target audience over their whole marketing plan. Trying to just reach your audience on Twitter or Facebook may seem like a good idea, but since there is so much competition on those platforms, it is much harder to actually reach your target audience. Instagram makes this easier because you have a large pool of target audience members, with a much lower number of industry competition to fight with.

Reaching your target audience

Instagram can make it easier for you to target the right audience. Each product has a target audience. This is the group of people you want to advertise your product to. These are the people you think are most likely to benefit from the product or the people who would be the most interested in using that product. If your target audience includes individuals who were born from 1980 to the early 1990s, or the group of individuals known as millennials, then Instagram is the best place to be.

The reason that Instagram is perfect for finding millennials is because it is believed that over 37 percent of the individuals in this age group are already active users on this social media site. This means that if you would like to reach out to and connect with this age group, then Instagram is the best place to find them.

Even if you are focusing on an age group that may be younger or older than millennials, you will find that Instagram can still work well for you. Brands like Red Bull, General Electric, and Ford have seen a considerable amount of success when they use Instagram. It is just about knowing your customer base, finding out where they are, and then catering to them there as well.

Free advertising

And finally, another benefit of working with Instagram is that it can help you to gain some free advertising for your business. The best thing about using Instagram is all of the free advertising that you are able to get. Think about it, if you are trying to sell something or promote yourself, you are going to fill up your page with a showcase of your services or products in action, which can generate a huge amount of exposure overall. This provides you with a chance to show off more of what you have to offer.

While there are some paid advertising and promotions that you can do with Instagram, there are also ways to promote your self and gain more followers and customers, all for free. This method can sometimes take longer, but as any business knows, free is always better on the budget.

Instagram is one of the best social media sites for you to choose in order to promote your business, beat out the competition, and really impress the customers you want to work with. The rest of this guidebook will take some time to explore more about Instagram and how you can set it up to get the most exposure, and the most potential profits possible with this great social media site.

Chapter 2: Tips to Set Up Your Instagram Account

Now that we know a little bit more about Instagram and how it works, and even some of the ways that it is going to benefit your business, it is time to go through and set up an account. You want to make sure that you do these steps in the proper manner and that you really put some thought and effort into it to ensure you get the best results. This is your brand, your business that you are promoting here, and making sure that you look and sound professional and that you get everything set up properly can be key when it comes to seeing results on Instagram.

How to Set Up a Business Profile on Instagram

Before you go in and create a new account for your business or if you already have an account, before you decide to refresh an old account, make sure to take some time and define the way that you want to use

Instagram in order to serve your business. This social media network can support a lot of different objectives for your business. But in order to make sure that you succeed with this business and marketing on Instagram, you must make sure that your focus is narrowed down a bit. In addition, you need to understand that consistency and content that is high-quality are so very important with this site.

When you make a business profile, there is a lot of extra information that you are allowed to add into the account. You can choose to include hours that you are open, an address for your business, and even a phone number, among other things, to make it easier for your customers to find you and get in touch with you when needed. If you choose, it is also possible to do paid advertising through Instagram and then get insights into how well the different stories and posts on your profile are doing.

There are just so many benefits that come with having a business profile on Instagram and it is definitely worth your time to give it a try and see how well your business can flourish. Some of the steps that you need to take in order to set up an Instagram Business

Profile include:

1. Download and then launch the app. This is available through Windows, Android, and iOS so you can use it on any system that works for you.

2. Tap the sign up button and enter in a phone number or email address to register. You also get the option to sign in with Facebook if you want to link the two together. You can then choose your username and then finish up the registration. When this is all done, sign into the app for Instagram through your phone.

3. Now you can go to the profile, or to the main page, and tap on the cogwheel icon. You can find this at the top right-hand corner of the screen. From here, you can click on the button that says "Switch to Business Profile" in your settings.

4. Tap on continue until you end up at the "connect the Facebook page" screen.

5. From this step, you can select the Facebook Page that links to your business and then link it back to your Instagram profile. One thing to note here is that when you do this process, you are only going to be able to view the pages that you are an admin of. You can also only link Facebook Business Pages in this manner.

6. Fill out the profile and make sure that everything is complete and filled out. Then you can start posting. As you get a few posts done, take a chance to analyze the success of each one with the help of different analytics Instagram provides.

Picking a Name

During this process, you will need to come up with a unique name for your page and this will become your username. You want to have something that relates back to your business but is unique and memorable enough that your customers will think of it when they try to look for you. Trying to fit in a few keywords that go with your business can help as well because it makes it more likely that people will find you if they do a search related to your business.

If you are a business that is up and running and has been for some time, you may just choose the name of your business as a username. This is easy for people to remember and if any of your customers are looking for you, it is probably what they will type into the search bar anyway.

But if you are a brand new business or you are an individual who is just getting started, you may not have a well-known business name yet. If this sounds like you, then it may be useful to think of something creative to put as your username. Pick out an option that is unique, something that stands out, and something that your customers, and potential customers, are going to remember.

Take your time when picking out a name. It doesn't look very professional if you are changing the name up on a regular basis for your page. You want a name that can grow with you, one that will impress others and really make you front of mind so your customers pick you first.

Polishing Up Your Profile

Make sure that when you work on your profile, the username, as well as the name you pick out for your account, match up with the business you are in, or even the industry that you participate in. Take some time to add in a description for the page. You are given 150 characters that you can use in order to describe what you and your business do, what that channel is for, and so on. 150 characters isn't a lot, so find a way to describe your self that is interesting and compact.

In addition, you should work on the bio section of the profile. This is where you should post a link to your website for the business. Links that go in individual posts aren't going to work well, so you should place it in the bio section. This helps your customers find out where they should go when they want to purchase a product or utilize your services. You can also update that link frequently, especially when there are special promotions, big product launches, and when you run an event.

Unlike what you will find with most of the other platforms for social media, Instagram is not going to come with the option to put up a custom cover picture to help with brand recognition. This means that the branding you do must come from all of the content that you publish on the profile, so you need to plan things out wisely.

Make sure to take a look around your profile and determine if it is complete and has all of the information that your customer would need. Pretend that you are a customer or have someone else do this and take a look at the profile. Will a potential customer know what kind of business you run? Will they know how to get to your website, how to contact you, or how to get their questions answered? Fill in any information that seems to be missing.

How Do I Get New Followers?

There are a few methods that you can use in order to gain more of the followers that you need. The more followers you get to your account, the more potential you have to turn them into customers and make a profit. But how are you supposed to get these followers?

The first option that you can use is to invite your current customers and followers from other social media sites over. If you already have a Facebook or Twitter account, let those followers know that you are now available on Instagram. Some may be interested in checking you out on there as well. Just make sure that you provide incentives and fresh content on Instagram that isn't exactly the same as what they can find on your other sites. No one wants to follow you on two or three sites and see the same information on each one.

If you have an email list of current and potential customers, mention the new Instagram account on one of your emails. This can alert your customers that you are now on that social media site, and some of them may be willing to check you out from there as well.

But in many cases, you may need to go through and do some legwork to help promote your page some more. First, you can go through and start following other pages. Look for pages that are similar to yours, ones that are in the same industry as yours, and ones that have interest similar to yours. Don't just like anyone, pick out ones that you actually find valuable.

It isn't enough to just comment on these pages though. You also need to go through and actively participate in them. Write out messages on the page, answer questions, and comment when you can. The more you can be involved on these pages and the more you interact with the page owner and the followers on that page, the more likely you will get a follow back, perhaps from the page owner and from some of their followers as well.

And finally, sometimes you will need to do some paid advertising and promotions to get your business page noticed by more followers. Instagram has a number of options when it comes to advertising that you can do. You can have a sponsored post, be listed in recommendations for users, and more. Take a look at each option to help you pick the right one.

Once you start gaining followers to your page, make sure that you interact with them and provide them with as much value as possible. Set up a posting schedule that is consistent and provides customers with content that is evergreen, pertinent, and valuable. Remember that Instagram is a great way to form relationships with your customers. Show them about your business, answer their questions, comment when needed, and more so you can build up the relationships that are needed to grow your business.

What Kind of Content Should I Publish?

When you are looking to grow your business through Instagram, you will be responsible for adding in a bunch of content on a regular basis. Even on Instagram, there is competition and your audience is bombarded with information and businesses all of the time. If you don't post on a regular basis, you will find that your customers will forget about you.

It is important to set up a strategy for your posts right from the beginning. The first thing to consider is the type of content that you will post. There needs to be some variation on the profile. You don't want to spend all of your posts showing the exact same product all the time. This gets boring pretty quickly and you won't have much time before customers turn away.

Instead, take the time to publish a variety when it comes to your posts. Talk about your products, talk about things that interest you, talk about what your business is doing, have surveys and contests, and more. The more variety that you can come up with, the better. Think outside the box and find ways that you can make your page interesting so customers keep coming back.

Another thing that you need to think about is times of posting your information. There is no magic number or magic time for your posting, but you want to make sure it is enough that your customers will see you daily and will come back and hear more news about you. The key here is to stay consistent. You can find the schedule that works the best for you and you can even schedule the posts ahead of time, but make sure that you have a plan in place so you are always on top of mind for your customers.

Starting your profile on Instagram doesn't have to be overly difficult. You just need to know how to set up the business account, how to post useful and valuable information to attract your customers, and how to find the right followers for your business. This can take some time and consistency to accomplish, but the companies who put in the effort will find that it pays dividends in terms of return on investment for their marketing.

Chapter 3: Creating Stories and Engaging with Your Audience Through Instagram

One neat thing that you are able to work on when you start your Instagram business account is Instagram stories. These stories are a feature inside of this platform that will allow individuals and businesses to publish videos and pictures that will be available to their followers for 24 hours. Unlike a regular post on Instagram, these stories won't appear on the newsfeed for any of your followers. Instead, these are going to appear right at the top of newsfeeds for your followers who want to take a look.

If you are ever interested in checking out the stories for other users, you simply need to click on the button to get back to your home page. From there, you will see that there is a little bar near the top that has profile pictures with a ring around it, pictures of those you are following. When you tap the picture, the story will play for you and the ring is going to disappear so you know that the story has been seen already.

These stories can be another great way for you to engage with some of your followers. Remember that engagement with your customers is so important to help them know that you value them and to keep them informed about the products and services that you offer. In addition, the more that you engage with your followers, the more likely that you are going to be able to see their stories right at the front of the line. And when they interact with you more, your stories are going to show up in front of you.

There are a lot of benefits that you can get for using these Instagram stories for your business. But before you use them, you need to have a goal in mind. The reason this goal is so important is because it is going to shape the content that you place in that story. You can choose from a variety of goals including turning your viewers of the story into subscribers, redirecting people to click on a link to your website, and increasing engagement.

The key here to ensure that you create a story that is engaging is to make sure that there is some structure to it, meaning that it has a start, a middle, and an end.

The first thing to consider is coming up with a strong start. If your movie starts out boring and doesn't catch the attention of your followers, then no one is going to stick around and listen to the rest of it. The beginning of your video needs to be enticing to your viewers so that they stay around to see how it is going to end. A good way to do this is to make a big promise in the first few minutes so people stick around to figure out what the promise is all about.

A good way to start out your story could include something like "I'll show you the number one fat burning food that can keep you fuller for longer and that tastes great." Or, another opening that you can use that is strong is to list out the types of people who should be watching the story, or who you planned this story for in the first place. So you could say things like "this story is for you if you've been yo-yo dieting and would like to finally get back in shape without spending hours at the gym and without starving yourself."

Once you have a strong beginning to your story, it is time to work on the middle. The middle needs to be high-quality as well. Since you are only going to have a little bit of time (these stories are very short), you will only have a few seconds or so to fill in the middle. You may have some room for two or three good tips or some good advice in the story.

And finally, make sure that the story you are working on has a strong end to it. Give the viewer something to do with the information that you provided them. Always include a good call to action. It isn't enough for you to just tell the viewer to click on your website or something similar. You need to spend some time emphasizing why it is so important for your viewers, why they should click on that link, and why it will benefit them.

Remember, these stories can only be 15 seconds long and then they are going to disappear after just 24 hours. This means they need to be impactful, even in the short amount of time with them. This is a great way for you to use the stories to help promote your business and reach your customers without having a lot of extra promotional posts cluttering up your profile and making a mess. But you must make good use of your time in these videos, otherwise, don't use them at all.

How Do I Figure Out Ideas for an Instagram Story?

Now that we know a little bit more about these stories, it is time to think of the ideas that your business will want to use in these stories. To collect the best ideas for stories, do a bit of research and see what other companies in your business have been successful with using. Then you can follow these profiles and see the stories when they come up. You don't want to copy, but you can use these for some inspiration. Some other ideas that you can add into your stories to make your stories stand out include:

- Show someone using your product or doing a task related to your business
- Show yourself talking directly to the viewer
- Create a collection of pictures being displayed in a slideshow format.
- You can create a video clip that has some subtitles that the viewer can look at
- Consider some background music that is impactful

You may notice that some of the stories that show up with the companies and individuals you follow are actually a compilation of many different short clips. This helps them make a video that is longer than the 15 seconds per story. But the key for your business is not to try to prolong the video, the key is less is more. When you make a story that is too long, it is possible that your viewers will lose interest. It is much better to keep the story short and sweet. At the most, have two videos together and get 30 seconds, but try to keep your videos as short as possible.

How to Enhance a Story on Instagram

There are many different methods that you can use to help enhance your stories on Instagram. You can choose to add in text, story filters by swiping left or right, put emojis into the story, and even adding stickers and using drawing tools. All of these are available in the menu for Instagram and are meant to ensure that your videos and stories are even more engaging with the potential customer.

But first, you need to be able to create your own story. To start with this, you should log into the business account that you have with Instagram and head straight to your home page. Look over to the left side of that home page and click on the part that says "create story". After you click here, you are going to choose from a few options. You can either take a picture when you click on the button that says "normal", or you can continuously press on that button in order to get the video clip to record instead. Then after you have the clip down, you can add in the filters and the other features as they work for the story that you create.

Instagram gives you the option to take some of the pictures that were taken on your phone over the past day, and then turn those into a story if you would like. Click on the camera and then do a swipe up so that you can see a list of all the pictures that you took within the last 24 hours. Then you can pick from those and turn them into a story that will entice your viewers.

This can be useful for several different reasons. For example, let's say the night before you went to a big event for your business and you want to turn them into a story that will show what the business has been up to and provide some entertainment to your customers as well. This story process from Instagram has made all of this a lot easier to handle.

Leveraging Your Business Account on Instagram

If you already have your business account, you will find that the Instagram story features are going to include swipe up for the story. With this feature, you now have the ability to write a "swipe up for link" on the story, rather than having to say the call to action. This ensures that the customer is able to get to your link really easily, which secures the sale for you better than ever.

Thanks to this swipe up feature that is allowed on Instagram story, people are able to automatically click on the right link and get redirected to your site or another location that you want. Instead of the customer having to go and search for the link through your bio, they can just click right on the story. This makes it so much easier, which is why you need to change your account over to a business one if you haven't done so already.

Always Check Into the Analytics

When you are using things like Instagram stories or some of the other features that come with Instagram, it is important to spend at least a little time looking at the analytics and how well these stories are doing. You are able to check out how popular these stories are by clicking on the eyeball symbol that is at the left-hand bottom of your page. This will tell you how many viewers were there to the story and even gives you their names so you can make sure to target them more later on.

When it comes to these stories, the viewers are not able to comment on them directly. Instead, the viewer either has to engage just by watching the story or they can choose to send you a personal message. Stories aren't available to be shared so it is hard for your customers to help you spread the word and they aren't able to like them either. You will have to look at the analytics often too since these stories are only going to stick around for 24 hours before they disappear.

Should I Include These Stories as Part of My Business?

There are a lot of different reasons why you should consider including these stories as part of your Instagram story. Some of the reasons that other companies and businesses are using these stories as part of their marketing plan include the following:

1. There are more than 300 million active daily users of these stories.

2. The average amount of time that Instagram users are on the platform is 28 minutes. This gives them plenty of time to see the stories that you post on your account.

3. More than 50 percent of the businesses that market on Instagram have spent time creating these stories and they have seen a lot of success. You should use it too.

4. 20 percent of the stories that are posted by companies will result in some kind of direct interaction with a user, which could easily turn into a sale.

5. More than 1/3 of users on Instagram are going to watch these stories each day. This is a ton of potential for you to reach your customers and get some great results with your advertising.

6. There are more than one million active advertisers each month who have seen some success using Instagram stories ads and you can benefit from this as well.

These Instagram stories are some of the best ways to reach out to your followers and turn them into customers. They are more engaging than some of the other posts that you can work with, but they are only going to last for a little bit so they won't clutter up your whole newsfeed all the time. Make sure that the stories you create and post are high-quality, get the attention of your followers, provide some value to them, and add in a call to action. If you can do this and post the stories on a consistent basis, you have a recipe for making your business as successful as possible.

Chapter 4: Tips About Posting on Instagram to Get the Best Results

When you are on Instagram, one of the things that you will need to focus on is the posting that you do on your profile. Most of your followers are going to take some time to read through your posts and check out what you are all about. If you have a lot of engaging and thoughtful posts, you are more likely to get someone to follow you in the end. This chapter is going to focus on some of the steps that you should take in order to get started with posting on your Instagram profile.

What Should I Post?

As a business, you must carefully plan out everything that you post on your page. Even as an individual who is trying to promote themselves or their own personal brand, the posts that you add to your page are really going to matter. You want to make sure that you are posting items that provide value to your customers, things that are unique and can stand out, and things that really relate to or showcase your values as a business.

There are a lot of different things that you can consider posting when it comes to your profile. Adding some variety can be helpful as well. You can post pictures of your products, add some shorter videos, do some Instagram stories, post about some of the employees, do a contest, and think outside the box to come up with other ways to engage with your followers and get them excited to see what you will post next.

When it comes to creating your posts, you can keep this pretty simple. The first thing that you want to concentrate on is finding a high-quality picture to showcase. Remember that the first thing people are going to see when they come to your page is that picture. You want to go with one that is relevant, high-quality (consider hiring a professional photographer if needed), and engaging and attractive so that your potential customers and followers are drawn into it the moment they see it.

From there, you need to add in a description. The description isn't going to be the main event, so having one that is shorter on occasion is not a big deal. Mix up the copy a bit though. You don't want all of your descriptions to just be a few lines long. Some copy can create a story to go with the picture, others may be short, and plenty will be somewhere in between. Just make sure the copy goes with the picture that you are presenting and that it can engage the customer as much as possible.

A good thing to do with the description is to ask the customer a question. You may ask them what they would like to see with some of your products, what their favorite product is, some of their favorite things to do during the holidays, and so on. Find some way to get the customer to interact with the post, which increases engagement and visibility for your page.

Another thing to include in here is a call to action. You always need to include this on anything that you do with your Instagram page. Once the customer has admired the picture and read through your description, what is it that you want them to do next? Do you want them to comment on something? Do you want them to check out your website? You can choose what you would like the customer to do but make sure that it is included in your call to action at the end of the description.

And finally, make sure that you include some hashtags with your descriptions. These are little tags that go with your description and will ensure that your customers can find you better. Any time someone does a search on Instagram that matches up with your page and matches with the hashtags that you add in, you will be in the search results for that.

You should aim to add in at least five hashtags, although more is better. You can fill up the page with hashtags, which can make it easier for people to find you. The best thing to do here is to think of various keywords that people may use when they are searching for your business or your products, and then use those as some of the hashtags that go with your posts.

Creating high-quality and engaging posts are critical to seeing success when you are on Instagram or any other social media platform out there. You should take some time to think through the posts that you make to help you come up with the best post ideas possible.

When Should I Post?

The time of day that you schedule your posts can vary depending on what works best for you. This is a case where you really need to have a good idea of your target audience and when they are most likely to be online. For example, if you are targeting stay at home mothers, you may find that posting in the morning and then posting during nap time is going to provide you with the best engagement. But if you are targeting college students, it is best to post later at night when these students are more likely to be awake.

You also want to try and post at a time when your competition isn't posting. If you do this, then you are able to reach the customer when no one else is there to fight with you for attention. This may be one of the ways that you determine when you will post. Take a look at the times when your competition post and then post at times when they are less likely to be there.

You may need to spend some time experimenting with the times. You can post at different times of the day for a month or so, and then look at your analytics and see when people seemed to respond the best. This will give you a good idea of two or three times when your response rate and engagement seem to be the highest, and you can add that into your schedule.

The important part here is to make sure that you schedule things and become consistent. Things don't always need to be at the exact time, but if you are horrible about posting and go for weeks without it, and then all of a sudden post a bunch of things, then you are consistent for a few weeks before dropping off again, your followers will have no idea what to expect from you. Over time, they will stop even checking in and you will lose all of the hard work that you already put in.

How Often Should I Post?

The next question that you may have when it comes to posting on Instagram is how often you should post on this social media site. This is often going to vary based on the type of business you have, how the other competition in the industry posts, and more. In addition, the amount of times that you post is going to depend on your own schedule and the types of things that you are trying to promote in your business.

The first thing to consider is how often do you need to get the message across. While studies have shown that posting more often is not going to really bother the customers that much and it hasn't been linked back to a huge decrease in the number of followers that you have, it is still not a good idea to post every half hour during the day. Not only may this clutter up the newsfeed of your followers, but what is so important to post about 48 times a day?

It is important to find a good number that you can be consistent with. Usually, doing it at least two or three times a day is ideal for most businesses. This allows them some time to get news out to customers and can ensure that they are top of mind at least a few times a day. But it doesn't get to the point of annoying customers or not bringing anything of value to the table because you post too often.

Just like with the timing of your posts, you may need to experiment and see what works the best for you. Maybe for one week try to post two times, and then the next week post five times, and then do a week at four times. Then take a look at your analytics and see what seems to work the best for what you are doing. If you find that your customers respond the best when you post three times a week, then this is what you should stick with.

Posting is an integral part of running your business on Instagram. There are other features that you can use, but your followers, as well as any potential customers that you may work with, are going to spend the majority of their time looking at your profile and checking out the things that you post. You want to make sure that you post high-quality posts, ones that will grab the attention of your customer and will keep them coming back for more. If you follow the tips that are in this chapter though, you will be able to write high-quality and professional posts that really showcase your work and engage with the customers.

Chapter 5: Secrets to Help You Grow Your Profile and Your Audience

When you first get started on Instagram, you may have a few followers. You may have some people who come from your email list, some followers from your other accounts, and some who just randomly find you when they are searching around the platform. But the truth is, your following in the beginning is going to be pretty small. Many people may not even know you are there. But if you want to extend your reach and get the most out of this platform, then you will need to spend your time learning how to grow your profile and get a larger audience or a larger following.

The good news is there are a lot of different ways that you can grow your audience and therefore your business with the help of Instagram. Let's take some time to look at some of the best secrets and tips that you can follow in order to get more followers to your business page.

Like and comment on posts in your niche

In one online conference, the CEO of Freshly Picked, Susan Petersen, spent some time talking about how she was able to take her Instagram account and grow it to 400,000 followers at the time (since then she has expanded her following to 800,000). Petersen states that when she was first getting started, she would spend hours each night looking through pictures on Instagram and liking them.

While this may seem like it takes a lot of work, it has worked for many other Instagram marketers in the past. Her advice for businesses and individuals who are trying to grow their reach is to go through and like about five to ten pictures on someone else's account. It is even better if you are able to go through and leave a genuine comment on the account and even follow that person before you leave.

What this does is gets your name out there so that others are able to discover you. First, the owner of the page is going to see that you spent some time on their page and they will want to return the favor. Then the

191

followers of that page will start to see your name pop up and it may pique their curiosity. They may check out your page and even decide to follow you, growing your reach even more from a few minutes of work.

The best way to do this is to find users that are in your niche. You can do this by checking out hashtags that go with your niche or view the followers of some of your favorite names on Instagram. However, make sure that when you do this, you show some genuine personality, rather than being spammy. People can tell when you are trying to use them or spam them, and they will ignore you in two seconds if they feel like that is what you are doing.

Come up with a theme for the pictures on your page

Some businesses have found success when they create a theme to go with their pictures. You can choose the theme that works the best for your business and what you want to do on the page. Write down a few words that you would like people to think about when they come to your page and then use those to help you come up with a theme. This helps to keep the whole page cohesive and looking like it is supposed to go together and can really seem inviting to your followers and any potential followers who are checking out the page.

Spend your time socializing

The most successful individuals and companies on Instagram are the ones that spend a lot of time socializing. The more that you can interact, engage with, and socialize with your followers, the better results that you will get. Make sure that you respond to any comments that are left on your page and spend time commenting and liking posts of other influencers in your industry.

When you are commenting, make sure to put some thought and effort behind the words that you say. Don't just leave a comment like "cute!", because this only takes two seconds and the other person will barely notice it. But don't spend time writing three paragraphs about your own business either, because this will come off as being really spammy. Leave comments that are genuine, ask questions, and encourage others to interact back with you.

Create your own hashtag and get others to use this too

This is a great way to help out your business because it can ensure that you gain a lot of new content for your own account, and it can build up a community that will really benefit you in the future. The first thing that you need to do here is to create a hashtag that is unique. Double check to see if it is already being used or not. You want to go with something that is unique, easy to remember, and hopefully relates back to your business in some way or another.

Once you have the hashtag created, you can ask your followers to use it. This is going to be successful if you have a specific purpose for the tag. For example, the company known as A Beautiful Mess will encourage their followers to use the hashtag #ABMLifeIsolorful on all of their happy and colorful pictures.

After some of your followers have started to use this hashtag (and make sure that you are using it as well), you can then repost these images from the followers. Make sure that you give the follower credit for the picture, but this provides

194

you with a lot of fresh content that you don't even have to think up. Not only is this method able to build up some community in your industry because you show your followers that you really appreciate their pictures, but it ensures that you get fresh content for your own account.

Try out a contest

Another thing that you may want to try out is running a contest. If you have a product that you can give away or something that you are willing to give away to help grow your business, then it may be a good idea for you to run a contest. There has to be a catch though. For example, for someone to have a chance of winning the contest, users need to repost a specific image and then tag you in the caption. Or you can invite your followers to use a special hashtag that you design and then use it on their own images.

If you feel like really expanding this out and getting other Instagram names on board, you can consider doing a giveaway. You can get on board with a few other profiles and influencers, and then everyone can be a part of this. This helps to give each profile or business a chance to reach new customers and can be a great way to build up your business like never before.

Don't forget those Instagram stories

We already spent some time talking about Instagram stories and all the cool things that you can do with them. But make sure that you actually take the time to use a few of these. You don't necessarily need to do one of these each day, but doing one each week or every few days, can really help you connect with your customers and your followers.

These short clips may not seem like much, but since most of your followers are going to be visual, they can make a big difference. Plus, these videos are more interactive and engaging than traditional posts, so they can help you there as well. Having a good mixture of good posts and stories can help that customer base grow faster than ever before.

Encourage your followers to take some actions

It may seem pretty simple, but you will find that your followers are more likely to do something if you actually ask them to do it, rather than just assuming they are going to do it for you. Are you sharing a quote with your followers? Then ask them to like the post if they happen to agree with it. Are you sharing something that is considered relatable or funny? Then ask your followers to tag some of their friends or share the post. Ask your followers some open-ended questions, have them share information about a contest, and find other ways to get the customer engaged as much as possible.

The reason that you do this is to promote some more engagement with the stories that you are doing. The more engagement you get, the higher your account will show up, and the easier it is for new and interested followers to find you. Always ask your followers to show some interest in your posts and you will be amazed at how much more they are willing to participate.

Add a geotag to your pictures

Another tip that you will want to try out is adding a geotag on your picture. There are a lot of different ways that you are able to do this and you are likely to find a lot of success when it comes to this. For example, if you just took a picture of a really cool new restaurant or a city that you traveled to, and then you decide to use that as one of your postings on Instagram, then take the time to geotag it.

When you add a geotag to your account, other people who used that same kind of tagging are able to see that picture as well. When they see that connection, they may be more willing to follow you because they already noticed that you both have something in common. It may seem like such a little thing, but that small connection is often enough to get people to start following your account. It is a simple thing to do and only takes you a few seconds, but you will be surprised at how many followers you can get with this method.

Learn what your followers actually like

It isn't going to do you any good to work on a bunch of posts if the things you post are turning your customers off. Remember, your customers have complete control over whether they are going to check you out or not. You must make sure that you are posting things that your customer actually likes. This encourages the followers to stay, gets them to share the information with others, and can get your followers to engage better.

To figure out what things your customers like the most, it is time to do some research. Go through all of those posts and pictures that you have on your profile and check out which ones ended up with the most comments and likes. You can also check out which ones had the least comments and like. This helps you to see what seems to click with your audience and then tailor your message and your future posts to that.

Link Instagram to some of the other social media sites you are on.

As a business owner, you probably have other social media platforms that you are going to be on. If you are on Facebook, Twitter, or even have a blog, then you may make the assumption that all of your followers are already following you on each of these platforms. But in reality, they are probably only following you on just one of these platforms.

To help increase the number of followers you have, make sure to send out a quick message on the other platforms you are on to let your followers know they can now follow you on Instagram. You may be surprised at how many followers you are able to get this way.

Approach other users that are popular in your niche and set up a collaboration

This is an idea that will ask you to think outside the box a little bit. Take some time to research a few of the other profiles in your niche and then talk to them about doing a collaboration. For this, you can ask them to talk you up or ask if you can take over their account as a guest contributor. You will find that doing an Instagram story takeover can be a lot of fun and can even grow your following in the process. In return, you let that influencer do the same on your page.

What this does is introduces both parties to brand new audiences, audiences that they may have never had a chance to meet without this opportunity. Both of you can benefit as followers hear the stories, learn about the other person, and decide to start following you. The more times you are able to do this, the bigger you can grow your audience.

As you get used to working with Instagram, you will find that the most important thing you can do is grow your audience. The more followers you are able to get to your page, the more potential customers you get to work with. Using some of the tips and secrets that we have above, you will be able to get more followers to your account in no time.

Chapter 6: How to Convert Your Followers into Buyers

Instagram has been a boon for a lot of different brands. It is a self-promotion safe space that allows a lot of companies to showcase their services and products in a way that hasn't been done on other platforms. But since this platform is going to be limited to mostly video sharing and pictures, without help from a click through e-commerce feature, the return on investment can be a bit harder.

While we have spent some time in this guidebook taking a look at how you can build up your list of followers and get more eyes on your products, it is now time to take this a bit further and explore how you are able to take these followers and turn them into some of your paying customers.

First off, realize that not all of your followers are going to become your customers. Some people may like looking at your products or hearing news about you, but they may not make any purchases. Others may be frequent shoppers with you. And others will shop on occasion or just once. But your goal is to turn as many of those followers into customers as possible. The good news is there are a few steps that you can take in order to make this happen and they include the following:

Make all of your followers on Instagram feel like they are in your inner circle

Even on social media, people want to feel included. One of the best ways to make the person feel like they are a part of your community, and therefore make them more willing to purchase from you, is to ensure that they feel like they are actually a part of your inner circle.

It is pretty common knowledge that a bit of incentive can go a long way when it comes to seeing a boost in your sales. And when it comes to gaining some traction on your social media platform, this is still true. In one study that was done in 2013, it was discovered that about 49 percent of Americans liked a Facebook page for some company or another because of loyalty. And then 43 percent would become a fan of a certain page in order to get special deals or coupons. The trick to making this one work is to find the sweet spot between those consumers who may just decide to follow you in the hope of getting a discount, and try to get them to stick around because they actually do like and support the products you sell. This is where your followers on Instagram are going to come in. These particular followers already have an interest in the products and brand you are presenting, but now you need to provide some incentive to get them to purchase from you.

One way that you can do this is to do a tease for an exclusive offer on the Instagram feed, one that the followers aren't going to be able to get in stores or online. This means that the special is only available to those who follow you on Instagram. This makes the followers feel special, and they may be willing to make a purchase, even if they hadn't been considering it before.

Not only is this strategy going to be a good one to drive some sales, but it ensures that the followers feel like they are on the inside. This proves valuable because they will have more goodwill for your brand.

When you use your Instagram business account as real estate for your promotions, it is easier to remind your followers to start shopping now, and that they should check back often to find more steals and deals as well.

Add in a call to actions to your posts and stories

Never do a post without some kind of call to action. This needs to be on your posts and on your stories. Your followers need to know what they should do next, and as we talked about, asking them is going to be more efficient than just assuming they know what you want them to do. This call to action can get rid of any confusion and will make it more likely that you get the sale.

When you work on a call to action, it isn't always going to be a call for the customer to purchase something. Maybe it asks them to like your page, use a hashtag, or even share or repost the thing you put up. But if you have an item that you are posting about and you want to sell, then your call to action must be about purchasing that item if you want to turn at least some of your followers into customers.

Turn the store into a hot spot

Thanks to some of the filter effects and features that come with Instagram, but this platform has a way to turn almost any picture and any item that you are promoting look pretty enviable. You have probably scrolled through the feed at least a little bit and wished that you had some of the items that were there. If you are promoting your own business on Instagram, why not make sure that all the pictures you are posting of your store have that same feel.

Many brands that happen to manage pop-up shops find that they are pretty good at promoting in-store events on their Instagram pages. For example, the online retailer that is known as Piperlime is constantly showing pictures of the yummy treats that they sell and they use imaging that shows off some of their pop up parties in order to get customers more interested as well.

Instagram is working on a buy now feature

One new feature that Instagram is releasing is the

purchase or buy now feature. This works similar to what is found on Pinterest and other social media sites, and it is going to lead to more followers deciding to click on the link and make a purchase as well.

Let's say that you are a store that sells shoes. You may have a sale on a pair of boots and you decide to list them on your past to promote the sale. With this new feature, you can add in a button that allows your followers to click on the link and purchase those boots. This takes some of the work out of your followers having to search for your link. And when the customer is able to click on the link right away, they are more likely to give in to impulse shopping and this leads to a sale for you.

Pay attention to the lead your fans have

Chances are that your products are out on Instagram, even if you don't have an account. This can happen when you have customers who are snap happy and excited about the products that you provide. The good news is that you can leverage some of the legwork that your customers already did and then use that work on your brands' page. This can save you time, shows off a positive review that you got from a customer, and can enhance the product because you provide a visual example of how to enjoy and use your product.

For example, on the Instagram of Ben and Jerry's, you will notice that most of the posts are going to be credited user pictures (remember to credit the follower or user when you repost their picture). Your mouth is going to water from all the good looking treats, but this profile basically just reposted pictures of their customers enjoying the snack.

When other customers get a chance to see that the product is popular, can actually see the product, and then get a chance to see how that product should be used, it can actually make the product seem more appealing. This is where that unique hashtag can come in handy as well. You can ask your customers to use that hashtag any time they post a picture of them using or wearing your product. You simply have to search that hashtag, then repost, and you have a lot of your work done for you, and a simple way to turn some of your followers into customers in the future.

The overall goal of collecting as many followers as

possible is to turn them into customers. It doesn't do you much good to have 10,000 followers on your business page if none of them ever actually purchase some of the products that you are selling. When you use some of the suggestions in this section, you will find that it is easier to take those followers and convince them to purchase your product.

Chapter 7: Using Paid Advertising on Instagram to Grow Your Reach Faster Than Ever

No matter the size of your business, advertising on Instagram can be a great experience. It allows you a chance to really get your content in front of potential followers so you can get the best results in no time. Instagram makes it easy to advertise with them, doing promotions and more so that you can see your business grow.

The methods that we have focused on so far in this book are mostly about growing your reach in an organic manner. This is very important for your business because it helps you to increase your exposure and your following with people who are truly interested in you, ones who were able to find you on their own and the growth was free. As a business trying to keep costs down as much as possible, finding a way to reach your customers that is free and won't eat up your budget can be one of the best things ever.

Despite all of the good that can come from the organic reach through Instagram, there are times when you may want to speed things up. Yes, you should still work on the organic reach that we talked about earlier because that will keep your marketing budget intact and will help you to gain an edge over the competition. But sometimes, you just need to add in some Instagram paid advertising to really ensure your message, and your business, are getting out there to the right customers.

All sizes of businesses should consider using Instagram as their way to promote themselves, whether they are trying to promote a product, a service, or a brand. Some of the reasons that you should consider using Instagram paid advertising, even if you are just an individual trying to get noticed on Instagram to make money, include:

1. Anyone is able to advertise and get some great results when they are on Instagram. As long as you learn how to set up the campaign in the proper way, you will be able to see results.

2. You are able to target audiences on Instagram with the data that you have from Facebook. Facebook owns Instagram now so you can integrate these two together to get even better results.

3. Your engagement with the audience is limitless. As a business, you can interact with your users in so many ways, and these advertisements make it even easier to do so.

4. The ads that you create will look just like the other pictures and posts that are already on Instagram. This makes them feel less obtrusive and can help you get more people to look at them.

When you are on Instagram, there are going to be six different formats that you will be able to choose from when it comes to making your own ads. Four are going to be Instagram feed ads, and then the others will be Stories ads. All of these can be pretty effective at growing your market, but you have to determine which ones are going to give you the biggest bang for your money. Let's explore each type of ad to help you make the best decisions for your business.

Instagram Feed Ads

The first types of ads that we are going to explore are the Instagram feed ads. These will include the carousel ads, slideshow ads, video ads, and picture ads.

Picture Ads

Picture ads can be a great place to start with your advertising to kind of get a feel for it and ensure that you learn more about your market. These single image ads will allow you to create a maximum of six ads, and each one will have just one image in it. Compared to some of the other ad types out there, these single image ads are going to be easy to make.

You first need to start out by selecting which pictures you would like to put into the advertising. You can go through the image library that you already have, or you can upload some new pictures just for this advertising. Or there is always the option of using some free stock images if you want to go with something new and different. Add in the picture and then choose the caption that you want to go with the ad.

For Instagram, you are able to have a caption that is up to 300 characters. Any of the text that you include that goes under the third line is going to show up as an ellipsis. The user simply has to click on this to expand it out and see the rest of what you wrote out. You can use the full 300 characters to write your ads, but Facebook usually recommends that you go with about 125 characters for them instead.

If you want the option for your audience to go directly to your site from the ad, you can click on the "add a website URL". Then enter in the URL to your website and select the call to action button. You are able to go through and ignore the other fields that are three, such as the description, headline, and display link because these aren't needed in your Instagram ads.

Video Ads

The next option that you can go with is video ads. These are going to contain either a GIF or a video for the single video ads. This can make your content a bit more interactive and engaging with the customer, and many advertisers like the return on investment that comes with this. You have to consider the product you are selling and then decide if a video ad is really the best way to showcase the work you want to show off.

Once you decide that the video ads are the right ones for you to use, you can choose your video or upload a brand new one that you just created. You can then choose which thumbnail picture you want to choose for the video. Facebook will offer you a few options, but often uploading one that is custom can ensure that you get the most attractive option for your advertising. If you would like to, it is possible to add in some captions for the video as well. Finally, upload an SRT file now.

The caption is not required, but it can help explain the video, gets some keywords in there to help you reach the right people, and you can even use some hashtags. Just like with the picture ads that we talked about above, you are limited to just 125 characters with these video ads. Then, if you would like the video to send some traffic to your personal website, make sure that you add in the URL to that website, and select that there should be a call to action button.

Slideshow Ads

You can also choose to work with slideshow ads. These are like a video ad, but they go in a loop and you can pick up to ten images with music. It is similar to the carousel ads that we will talk about later, but it will be able to scroll on its own without the potential follower having to do the work.

Creating these ads doesn't have to be difficult. You can either go through the library of pictures that you have on your account and use those, or you can create a brand new slideshow. Facebook Ads Manager allows you to use the slideshow creator in order to make your own slideshow with the pictures that you want to use. If you create a slideshow, you just need to upload your images, arrange them, adjust the settings, and then pick the music that you want to use.

Make sure during this that you choose a good thumbnail that will showcase what is in these ads, and then add in the caption and website URL so you can get some conversions along the way. You even have the option of taking some of the posts that you put on Facebook and use these for your Instagram ads. This can work well if you already have some posts that were on Facebook that did pretty well performance wise in the past.

Carousel Ads

Another option available to you is the carousel ads. These are going to be ads that have at least two but can have more images or videos attached to them. This is a great way to showcase a few of your videos that were popular, or even a series of products that go together well that you are trying to sell.

Just like with the other options, this one is easy to do. For this, you need to pick out the videos or the pictures (known as cards) that you want to have in the ad. You are allowed to put a maximum of ten cards into one of these ads. For every one of these cards, pick out a slideshow, video, or image that you want to go into it. You can choose to have just one card filled up, or you can have up to ten for your advertising.

Once the cards are filled up, you should add in a

217

headline, which will be the first line of the caption. You can choose to make this the same or different for each card that you made. It is often best to leave the description blank here, outside of adding in the URL destination for your call to action button.

The next thing that you will notice here is that you need to keep the See More Display URL and See More URL blank. These are used for other types of ads but won't work the best for these carousel ads. Choose the call to action button that is the best for all the images. This call to action is going to appear the same on all of them, so don't post up pictures that need a different call to action because it just won't work.

Now, before we move on, there is one more thing that you need to consider having with all of your ads on Instagram. And these are some lead forms. No matter the format of the ad that you are going to run on Instagram, you must create a lead form to help out. You can use one that you may be using for other purposes, or you get the option to make a brand new one if that works the best. If you are looking to make one of your own for Instagram, some of the fields you must fill in to make this happen includes:

1. Welcome screen
   a. Headline
   b. Image
   c. Layout
   d. Button text
2. Questions
3. Privacy policy
4. Thank you screen
   a. Make sure that this page also has a link for your website so that people are able to head over there and visit when they complete the form.

Once you have been able to complete these fields, you can click on Finish to complete that lead page. You can also choose to click the Save button if you want to come back to this later. The lead page only has to take a few minutes to complete, but you will find that it can really help you to learn more about your customers and get insights into what works and what doesn't. While you may have a lot of questions to ask your customers, make sure this lead page is kept to a minimum so you can get useful information, without irritating the customer and making them leave before a purchase.

Ads with Instagram Stories

The four methods that we talked about above can be really useful when it comes to reaching more customers. If you pick good videos and good pictures, and you use engaging content and descriptions, you will be able to get a lot of conversions that result in more profits for you. But as a business, it is important to always look for new and innovative ways that you can reach your customers, and this means finding unique ways to advertise on Instagram as well. This is where the Instagram Stories ads.

Recently, Instagram decided to open up these ads to business and individuals throughout the world. These particular ads are going to appear right in between the stories that show up for your followers and potential followers. There are going to be two formats for these ads right now, mainly the single video and the single image. It is possible that this could change in the future as more businesses use it and you will have more options to make this work for you.

Single image

First, we are going to take a look at the single image. With this kind of format, you can make up to six ads just by working with one image in each one. Each ad is going to look just like a Story post on Instagram, but the difference is that there will be a small text of "Sponsored" that shows up on the bottom. This helps them to blend in well with some of the other stories and still gives the customer a choice on whether they want to view it or not. But if you do a good job, your potential customers will be ready to take a look at your products.

The ads that come with Instagram stories are pretty easy to do. You just need to go through and upload the images. You can then set in some information on your target audience and the demographics that you want to work with, set the budget that you are willing to spend, and then send it out. You can also work with pixel or offline tracking by going to the Show Advanced Options and changing up the selections.

Single video

You can also do a single video ad format through Instagram Stories. With this kind of format, you will be able to upload a GIF or video that is no more than 15 seconds long. Then you can promote it on your profile and to other potential users to learn more about your products or about your company.

To create one of these, you need to upload the video or the GIF that you want to use. You can select the thumbnail that you want to use for this. Remember that the thumbnail is going to be the image that people will see before the video is played, so pick one that helps showcase the material in the video, one that is clear and easy to see, and one that is high-quality. You can then enable both offline tracking and pixel by clicking on "Show Advanced Options" before the ad goes live.

How Much Do These Ads Cost?

As a business, it is important that you pay close attention to your budget. Even though Instagram can be very successful, you have to be careful that you aren't spending more money then you need to on marketing through this platform. Since the ads on Instagram are going to work with the same system that you saw with Facebook Ads, many marketers assume that the two are going to cost the same for them.

However, there can be some differences in prices. The cost of an ad on Instagram is going to depend on the amount you place in your budget and whether you are interested in automatic or manual budding. The good news is that according to many experts in the field, including Timothy Masek, the senior growth strategist at Ladder, running an ad on Instagram is two times or more cost-effective compared to running ads on Facebook.

So, if you have spent some time advertising on Facebook in the past, you already have a good idea of what budget you have to set to get a certain type of result. But when you switch things over to Instagram, your results could be twice as effective for the same budget. This is great news for businesses, no matter what their size is.

Of course, there isn't an exact figure available to tell you what the ad is going to cost on Instagram. However, the typical CPM for one of your Facebook Ads usually falls around $10. But on Instagram, that typical CPM is going to be around $5. This number can be higher or lower based on the type of customer you would like to reach.

Always remember that the ads you do on Instagram are never going to cost more than you are willing to spend. If you set a budget that is at $10 each day, the platform is never going to charge you higher than this figure. Think carefully about how much you want to spend on your ad campaign and how much you are willing to pay for the advertising each day. This number will be different for each company and can depend on your audience size, the amount of budget you have available, what kind of goals you are trying to meet, and so much more. But having this budget set out ahead of time can make a big difference in keeping you on track.

Many businesses choose to work with paid advertising on Instagram. This helps to speed up the results they get with followers, customers, and attention on the site. Doing this along with some of the organic reach that we talked about earlier can really ensure that you grow your page, reach more people, and see the results that your business is looking for. Before moving on to the next chapter, take some time to explore more about the different ad formats that are available from Instagram and decide which one may be the best for you.

Chapter 8: Setting Up Your Ads and Promotions on Instagram

The first thing we need to look at here is how to set up an ad on Instagram. This process is going to be pretty simple, but for each ad that you decide to do, make sure that you take your time and really go through each of the parts. This will help you to reach the right customers, set a budget that is going to be effective, and create content that is high-quality and will really reach your customers where they are right now. Let's look at some of the steps that you can follow when you are ready to set up your ads and your promotions through your Instagram account.

Choosing your target audience

Just like Facebook Ads work the best when you spend time setting a target audience, Instagram Ads are going to work in a similar fashion. The more specific you can be with this target audience, the more efficient your budget will be in the end. You can target your audience by picking from several different factors including languages, connections, interests,

226

gender, demographics, behaviors, age, and location.

Depending on your goals with this advertisement, you may also want to consider targeting people who have, at one point or another, interacted with your content or people who have some form of connection or relationship with your current customers. Once you set these criteria, you can start to target other people like these users with the help of a tool from Instagram known as the Lookalike Audience.

Once you have taken the time to select all of the targeting options (and be as specific as possible here because this will increase your chances of finding the right people), Facebook Ads Manager through Instagram is going to reveal a bunch of information to you that can help with you knowing whether the ad is going to be successful or not. Some of the information you can look through after picking out all the targeting options include:

1. Potential reach
2. The daily reach the system estimates based on your criteria
3. How specific or broad the audience is
4. The criteria that you set when doing targeting

Choose the placement of the ads

The next thing that we need to take a look at is the placement of your ads. This is important, especially if you want to do the ad on Instagram and Facebook together, or you want to do a feed ad and an Instagram Stories ad at the same time.

Now, it is possible for you to go through and choose just to run the ads on Instagram. If you want to do that, we can do it right now. Go into "Edit Placements" and then make sure that under the platforms you have deselected Facebook. If you want to do an ad for Instagram Stories, you can go into your account and select "Stories" from your drop-down menu (it will be on the left of the screen).

From here, you are able to use some advanced options in order to pick out the specifics that you want to go on with your ads. For example, you may want to select the operating system and even the devices you would like these particular ads to go to. In some cases, it doesn't matter and you will want the marketing to occur on all devices. But if you are a company who is marketing a mobile app and that app only works on iOS, then this feature can really make a difference. Just go in and choose which devices you would like the ads to go to.

Check and see if there are any other targeting or placement options that may be useful for you. Instagram is always updating to provide the best service to their customers. You may be surprised by what you are able to find if you just take a look around the site.

Pick out your schedule and your budget

For this one, it is time to select how much you are willing to spend on the ads and how long you want these ads to run for. Depending on your needs, you may want to choose a lifetime budget or simply a daily budget. With the daily budget, you will list out the average cost that you are willing to spend on these ads each day. With the lifetime budget, you will set some dates in place for when the ad starts and when it ends, and then list out the total cost that you are willing to spend for the lifetime of the ad. You get the choices of having the ad run continuously until the total budget amount is reached or you can go through and actually set a start and end time.

You may also notice that there are some advanced options that you should look at to help with customizing your budget and your schedule to get the most out of your time and money. As a beginner, you may find that for the first campaign, you should just stick with the recommendations that Facebook offers and keep the default in place. As you get more used to the system and have some time to look through the different analytics to see what is doing well and what isn't, then you can make adjustments and change up some of the advanced options to work the best for you and your spend.

How can I lower my costs?

While Instagram is more influential and more effective with paid advertisement than you will get with Facebook and a number of the other social media platforms, you still want to work to keep your budget as low as possible so you can earn more profits or use that money in other places. If you are searching for a fast way to lower the costs of these ads, consider searching for a good Instagram influencer.

Once you have been able to find this influencer, tag them in one of your posts or you can reach out to them and question whether they are able to promote your brand with you. One tool that you can use in order to find the influencers that you need is to work with Ninja Outreach. To use this, you just need to type in a keyword or two that is in your niche or industry, and you will be given a list of Instagram influencers to consider.

You can also slowly work through and gain some followers on your own. The more that you are able to do on your own would be commenting on posts, talking and interacting with your customers, and more. This process does take a bit longer than what you may be used to with the paid promotions, but they can reduce your costs a little bit.

Instagram is considered one of the biggest social media networks out there, besides Facebook. What this means for you is that there are endless opportunities for you to reach out to your customers, engage with them, and see some results in the end. There are already companies in every niche, including yours, who are putting their time into Instagram ads, which means you should be doing it as well. This chapter spent some time exploring how you can do this and get the most out of each and every ad that you decide to post.

Chapter 9: Things to Consider to Make Your Instagram Ads More Effective

When it comes to working on an Instagram Advertisement Campaign, you want to make sure that you are getting an effective ad post out to your customers in the most efficient way possible. You want to ensure that the right people are going to see it, that you aren't spending more money than you need to, and that you are going to gain as many conversions. Some of the steps that you can take to make this happen include:

Make them engaging

Even with just pictures and short videos, it is important to make your content more engaging. You want people to interact with you, comment on the advertisements, leave their opinion, share, and just engage with you as much as possible. This is part of the point of advertising. You want to get your message

233

out to as many people as possible and engagement makes this happen easier than anything else.

The way that you do this is going to vary depending on which industry you are in, what products you are trying to sell, and what you hope to get out of the customer in the end. The posts that you do promoting your business are going to be different compared to the ones for brand recognition, promoting products, and more. Try to think outside the box so you can really find ways to engage your customers in ways that your competition isn't doing.

In addition, make sure that you add that call of action into the end of every post, whether it is a regular post on your page or you are doing an advertisement. This helps the customer know exactly what they should do at the end of it all. The call to action doesn't always have to include a link back to your website, although it could. Simply asking the audience to share the post, to comment, or even like your post can work as a call to action as well. But no matter what, ensure that call to action is there right from the beginning.

Pick high-quality pictures and videos

Don't just slap up the first picture that you can find and make it your full campaign. There is so much visual content on Instagram, from good pictures to videos and more, that you really need to find ways to stand out from the crowd if you want any chances of your advertisement being effective and seen by your target audience. If you put up pictures that have nothing to do with your message or your business, pictures that are blurry or hard to see, or pictures of something boring like just your logo, you are simply throwing money down the drain when it comes to your Instagram promotion.

When picking out the pictures and doing the videos that you want to advertise with, think about what you would want to see from a business before you clicked on them. What would get your interest? What would get you to engage with the content? What would be something fun, something unique, something interesting that would make it easier for you to get someone to pay attention to you?

Always remember that there are a lot of other companies and business in the world, and they are competing for a lot of the same competition that you are. Submitting pictures and videos that are lower in quality and not taking the time you need to make a fantastic marketing campaign, even on Instagram, is going to hurt you a lot.

Always watch the analytics

It is never a good idea to make an ad or a promotion, post it on Instagram, set a budget, and then ignore it. You put so much effort into all of the steps, why would you just let it go and not pay attention to how it performs? How do you know if you have set the right budget? How do you know if you are spending too much or too little? How do you know if your followers or potential customers are actually responding to the ad at all?

Analytics help you to answer all of these questions or more. And any time that you have a campaign up and running, you need to take the time to check in on these analytics at least once a day. If the campaign is really long term and you have ironed out the kinks, you may be able to reduce this. But as a beginner who is learning the ropes and for short term campaigns, your analytics are going to be your best friend to ensuring you know exactly how an ad is doing and it will help you to get the most profitable and efficient promotion possible.

Instagram offers a variety of analytics tools that you can use, it is a good idea to use as many of them as possible. You can then make changes to your promotions as needed, add more to the budget, lower your budget, try out a different advertising type, try out different pictures, and more. Even with a lot of research, it is sometimes hard to know what is going to click with your customers. Using the analytics from Instagram can make this job easier.

Set your budget and time frame

We talked about setting your budget a bit in the last chapter, but it is important to get this set and ready to go right from the beginning. As someone who may be brand new to Instagram, or at least new to promoting a business on Instagram, it is hard to know how much you should budget. Of course, you want to keep the budget low so you don't spend more than necessary, but you also want to make sure your budget is high enough that you are actually getting the message out to the right people in an effective manner.

If you are uncertain about the amount that you should put in your budget, then start out with a smaller number and build up from there until you find your sweet spot. This is where those analytics come into play. You can change the daily budget numbers until you see that you are getting the best return on investment. Once you have that number, you can set it at your budget while doing a scheduled campaign or leave it open-ended so the campaign keeps going.

You also have to decide if you want to set a time limit for the advertising campaign. Is this a limited time promotion? Do you only want to spend the daily budget for a few weeks or a month? Then you need to set a time limit on it. Instagram allows you to set a start and end date on all of your campaigns so this is an easy thing to work on.

You can also just leave the start and end dates blank. If you are just promoting your products or your

238

business as a whole, then maybe you want to keep the campaign open for now. You can always change the dates later or end the campaign when you feel it has run its course. But this option allows you to keep advertising the campaign without any stops until you change it up later on.

Try A/B testing

Sometimes when you are first learning the ropes of Instagram and what your customers may like or dislike, it is hard to know which direction to go. Or maybe you have two really good ideas, but you can only advertise one right now, and you want to know which one is the best idea for you. When these situations and more come up, working with A/B testing may be the best idea to help you out.

With A/B testing, you will take two ads, sometimes they are pretty similar with slight differences between them, and other times they are completely different because you want to see which campaign or idea is the best. Then you give them both a smaller budget for a week or two and see how they do. During this time, you watch the analytics and see which one is resulting in more conversions, engagement, likes, reposts, and more.

At the end of the trial run, you pick out the one that seems to be doing the best for you and that becomes the ad you focus on. The other one gets removed and the budget is moved over to the winner. You can then continue advertising this choice, but with a larger budget and get more followers and hopefully some more customers as well.

This method is a great one because it helps to take out the risk. You get a chance to try out two options to see which one is going to get a bigger response from your customers, without having to worry about spending twice the budget or sending out the wrong campaign in the first place. You can stick with the same budget you were planning on for one ad, just split it up, or you can pick out a smaller budget to do this.

Whether you are trying to grow your reach organically or through paid advertising and promotions on Instagram, it is important to pay attention to what is going on with your work, to look at what seems to be connecting with your customers, and always pay attention to any changes that may occur on Instagram, in your industry, and more. If you can do that and use the tips in this chapter and previous chapters, you are going to come up with a campaign that will easily increase your followers and your customers.

Chapter 10: Different Ways to Make Money on Instagram

One of the neat things about Instagram is that there are a lot of different ways that you can earn money through this platform. While this guidebook has spent a lot of time talking about how businesses can grow their following and earn customers, the same tips can be used for individuals who are looking to earn money online. A business may decide to just sell their own products online to customers and make a profit that way, but there are other methods that small businesses (depending on who they are) and individuals can use to earn a very nice income online from all the hard work they have done to gain followers and a good reputation on this platform. Let's take a look at some of the different ways that you can potentially make money on Instagram.

Affiliate Marketing

The first option is to work as an affiliate marketer.

Basically, with this option, you are going to promote a product for a company and then get paid for each sale. This is something that is really popular with bloggers because they work on getting their website set up, and then they can write articles about a product, or sell advertising space, and then they make money on any sales through their links. You can do the same thing with Instagram as well.

When you want to work with affiliate marketing with Instagram, you need to post attractive images of the products you choose and try to drive sales through the affiliate URL. You will get this affiliate link through the company you choose to advertise with. Just make sure that you are going with an affiliate that offers high-quality products so you don't send your followers substandard products. And check that you will actually earn a decent commission on each one.

Once you get your affiliate URL, add it to the captions of the posts you are promoting or even in the bio if you plan to stick with this affiliate for some time. It is also possible to use the bitly.com extension to help shorten the address or you can customize your affiliate link. It is also possible for you to hook up the Instagram profile and blog so that when people decide to purchase through the link at all, you will get the sale.

If you have a good following on Instagram already, then this method of making money can be pretty easy. You just need to find a product that goes with the theme of your page and then advertise it to your customers. Make sure that the product is high-quality so that your customers are happy with the recommendations that you give.

Create a Sponsored Post

Instagram users that have a following that is pretty engaged have the ability to earn some money through the platform simply by creating sponsored content that is original and that various brands can use. To keep it simple, a piece of sponsored product through Instagram could be a video or a picture that is going to highlight a brand or a specific product. These posts are then going to have captions that include links, @mentions, and branded hashtags.

While most brands don't really need a formal brand ambassadorship for the creators of this kind of content, it is pretty

244

common for some of these brands to find certain influencers to help them come up with new content over and over again. However, you must make sure that the brands and the products that you use are a good fit for the image that you worked so hard to create on Instagram. You want to showcase some brands that you personally love and can get behind. Then you can show the followers that you have how this brand is already fitting into your lifestyle so they can implement it as well.

Sell Pictures

This one is one that may seem obvious, but it can be a great way for photographers to showcase some of the work that you do. If you are an amateur or professional photographer, you will find that Instagram is the perfect way to advertise and even sell your shots. You can choose to sell your services to big agencies or even to individuals who may need the pictures for their websites or other needs.

If you are posting some of the pictures that you want to sell on your profile, make sure that each of them has a watermark on them. This makes it hard for customers to take the pictures without paying you first. You can also use captions to help list out the details of selling those pictures so there isn't any confusion coming up with it at all.

To make this one work, take the time to keep your presence on Instagram active. This ensures that the right people and the right accounts are following. This is also a good place to put in the right hashtags so that people are able to find your shots. You may even want to take the time to get some engagement and conversations started with big agencies in the photography world who can help you grow even more.

Promote Your Services, Products, or Business

As we have discussed in this guidebook a bit, if you already run a business, then Instagram can be a good way to market and promote your business. For example, if you already sell some products, use Instagram to post shots of the products, ones that the customer can't already find on your website. Some other ways that you can promote your business through Instagram include:

- Behind the scenes: These are very popular on Instagram. Show your followers what it takes to make the products you sell. Show them some of your employees working. Show something that the follower usually won't be able to see because it is unique and makes them feel like they are part of your inner circle.

- Pictures from your customers: If you pick out a good hashtag and share it with your customers, they will start to use it with some of their own pictures. You can then use this content to help promote your business even more.

- Exclusive offers and infographics: You can take the time to market your services through Instagram with some exclusive offers and infographics of your products. This works really well if the offers are ones the customer wouldn't be able to find anywhere else.

Sell Advertising Space on Your Page

If you have a large enough following, you may be able to get other brands and companies interested in buying advertising on your profile. They will use this as a way to gain access to your followers in order to increase their own followers, sell a product, or increase their own brand awareness. This is the perfect opportunity for you to make some money from all the hard work that you have done for your own page.

There are many different ways that you can do this. You can offer to let them do a video and then post it as your story, promote a post on your profile, or use any of the other ad options that we discussed above. You can then charge for the type of space they decide to use, the amount of time they want to advertise for, and how big of an audience you are promoting them in front of.

Become a Brand Ambassador

This is something that is becoming really popular with MLM companies. There is so much competition on Twitter and Facebook that many are turning to use

Instagram as a new way to promote their products and get followers that they may not be able to find through other means. And because of the visual aspects of the platform, these ambassadors can really showcase some of the products through pictures and videos.

There are many companies that you can choose from when it comes to being a brand ambassador. Since you have already taken some time to build up your audience and you have a good following, so if you can find a good product to advertise to your followers, you can make a good amount of money. You have to pick out a product that your followers will enjoy, ones that go with the theme of your profile to enhance your potential profits.

As you can see, there are many different options that you can choose from when you want to make some money through your Instagram account. All of the different methods make it perfect no matter what your interests are. After you have some time to build up your own audience and you have quite a few followers already looking at your profile and looking to you for advice, you can leverage this in order to make some money through this social media platform.

Chapter 11: Tips to Get the Most Out of Any Instagram Profile

Now that we have spent some time looking at the different ways that you can get your profile started, the benefits that you can get with Instagram, some of the organic ways that you can grow your business, and the best ways to use paid advertising and promotions on Instagram to really see results, it is time to move into some of the best tips to get even more out of these accounts.

Instagram can be one of the best ways for small businesses and even individuals to promote themselves, sell products, and even earn a nice income. If you want to make sure that you are able to really stick out from the competition and see some results with your work and the page, make sure to check out the tips below to help you out.

Always include a call to action

No matter what kind of posting you do, whether it is a

traditional post, an Instagram Story, or one of the different advertising types that we discussed, always make sure that there is some kind of call to action on it. Your customers need to have some idea of what you would like to do. And sometimes the best way to get your followers to listen to you or do something, you just need to ask them to do it.

There are a lot of different calls to action that you can consider going with. And the one you pick will often depend on the overall goals of that post. You may just want to spread the news about your company or your brand, and so the call to action would be asking your followers to share your information or repost some of the information. If you want the follower to purchase a product or visit your website, then your call to action needs to include the website URL so the customer knows where to go.

If you are uncertain what kind of call to action needs to be on the post, then it is time to revisit your goals. What are you posting this post for? What are you hoping to gain when this post goes live? Once you have the answer to this, you will be able to come up with the call to action that works the best for that post and for your business.

Start a consistent posting strategy

Posting on Instagram can be tricky. There are a lot of variables that you have to consider. You have to decide what times you want to post at. You have to decide what content you want to post on the page. And you have to decide how many times you would like to post on the page. Each company is going to have a different posting strategy that works for them. But the number one thing that you can concentrate on when it comes to this is coming up with a posting strategy that is consistent.

Consistency is key no matter which social media platform you decide to work with. You are never going to see results if you can't post your content on a regular basis. If you post a bunch for a month, and then go with just one posting a week, and then back to two posting a day, and then you go silent for three months, and so on, you will find that it is really hard to maintain the following that you want on the profile.

Your followers want to feel that there is some consistency to your posting. They don't want to feel like you are just using them to make money and then disappearing once they purchase from you or once you get bored with the whole thing. Figure out what kind of schedule not only gets the best response from your followers but also works the best for you and then stick with that. Over the long term, this will give you the best results.

Interact with your customers

Interaction is the number one thing that you can do when you are on Instagram or any other social media platform for that matter. Instagram is set up to be really interactive and if you aren't commenting and messaging and talking to others, then you are really missing out. The good news is there are a lot of different ways that you are able to interact with your customers while on Instagram.

The first way that you can interact with them is through the posts that you put up on your profile. Make the posts that you use as engaging as possible. Showcase the information that you want them to see, let the products do the work, do behind the scenes pictures, and utilize all of the cool features that you can get from working with Instagram Stories.

Then, when your customers start to comment, like, and repost on your posts, take the time to respond back. You don't have to spend all day on the computer to do this, but set aside a little bit of time each day, either in the morning or in the evening when you can go through and respond to as many followers and their comments as you can. In the beginning, this number probably won't be very big and you will only need to spend a few minutes on it. But as the number of followers to your page grows, you may need to manage your time well to answer and respond to as many comments as possible.

From there, you can engage in other ways as well. Find a few other profiles that are in your niche or that interest you and start following them. Leave some meaningful comments behind when you are done looking through and answer some questions if you are able to. If you can do this on a few different pages each week and slowly grow on this, you will be amazed at what it can do for you. The followers of those pages will start to see you, may get interested and check you out, and they may choose to become your follower as well.

The more that you are able to interact with your followers and with other pages on Instagram, the easier it is for you to grow your business. This gets more eyes on your profile and can make it easier for you to sell the products or the services that you want.

Schedule some automatic posting when you are busy

It is usually best if you can provide posts that are fresh and done right at the moment. This ensures that you can keep the posts interesting and relevant to that moment. If something new comes up with the business, you can always talk about that as well during the posting time that you set aside. Plus many times, the posts that you schedule ahead of time can sound a bit stilted and hard to read through and your followers are not going to respond well to that.

But there are times when you can get busy. You may not have time to post when you are running your business, traveling, and doing other day to day things. On occasion, when you know ahead of time that you will be busy for one or two days, it is fine to schedule the posts to go ahead automatically for you. This ensures that you can still reach your customers.

If you use this method, take some time to go back when you have a bit of time and engage with your followers. If they commented on the posts or asked questions, make sure that you communicate back with them. Just because you have these automatic posts doesn't mean that you now get to sit back and be lazy about the work. Your followers still expect to hear from you on a regular basis, so don't disappoint them.

Keep track of the analytics

Never forget to spend time looking at the analytics of your page and how your posts are doing. It doesn't matter if you are brand new to marketing on Instagram or have been on the platform for some time, there are always things that you can learn about your customers.

As a beginner, you will be able to use these analytics to learn what is good for your business and what your followers are responding to. Many beginners are not sure what they should focus on when they first get started. Do their customers like Instagram Stories or do they like posts with lots of good pictures? Do they like to see things that happen behind the scenes or do they like to just see pictures of how the products are actually used by the staff? Do they like to see a bunch of posts during the day or do they like to just see one or two posts during the day?

The best way to figure out what is working well for your business is to look at the analytics. You can see information on what posts your followers are paying attention to, what they are commenting on, engaging with, liking, and even reposting. You can then use this information to create your own marketing plan with more of the posts that your followers will respond to.

In addition, even after you have spent some time on Instagram and you have a good idea about what your followers like, it is still a good idea to keep track of these analytics. You never know when something new is going to look interesting and you will want to try it out, and looking at analytics can help you determine if this is going to be successful or not. And maybe the perception of the followers changes as you gain more and more, and you may need to change up your strategy as well.

Stay true to your brand

There are a lot of different things that you can do when you get on Instagram. You can reach your customers in a wide variety of ways and this can be exciting. But no matter what you do along the way, make sure that you are always true to your brand.

Your followers come to you for a reason. They want to learn about your business, see your products, and learn the personality that goes with your business. This is the beauty of social media, you can connect with your customers by creating a brand personality that your followers can look to and come to expect. When you try something that is completely different from your brand or your personality, it can easily turn off your customers and can make it hard to maintain the image that you want.

Let's say that you are a brand that is meant for families. You spend your time talking about some of the best things that families can do together on the weekend or for vacation and you sell products that go along with this. The followers you have accumulated are parents who are looking for ideas of what to do during vacation or who are just looking for products for their families. They go to your profile because they enjoy seeing your new products, getting advice on traveling with families, and more.

But what if you tried to change up your advertising all of a sudden? Maybe you start talking about the best spring break hangouts by the beach and showed pictures of sororities and fraternities partying all the time? What if your page became all about political posts and quit talking about family-related stuff at all? This goes off your brand and is something completely different than what your customers are looking for. Many will start to leave and this takes away all the hard work you did.

Post more rather than less

There isn't really a set amount of times that you should post on your profile. Some people find that two or three times a day is good, others may post once a day, and others may do five or more times. You really need to go with the schedule and the number of times that work the best for your own business. And this may take some experimenting to see what works the best. Maybe try out with one time a day and then build up. This makes it easier for you to see what works the best and what doesn't.

Studies have shown that there aren't a set number of times that you need to post. You don't need to post every few minutes, but posting more times, rather than less, can result in your customers being able to find you and keeps you front of mind with your potential customers. Find the number of times for posting that seems to work the best for you and then stick with that.

Instagram is a great platform for business and individuals alike. Individuals like to spend their time meeting up with friends and learning more about the brand and products they like. Businesses get a boost because they can engage and interact with their customers in a way that other platforms just aren't able to do. When the two come together, you are going to find that it can be a great thing on both sides.

Chapter 12: Case Studies of Success on Instagram

Instagram has the power to bring success to a lot of different business types. Whether you are a larger business or one that is smaller, you will find that Instagram has the results that you need to really see some success. This chapter is going to focus at looking at some of the success stories that have been made thanks to Instagram, as well as some of the steps and tools these companies used in order to reach their success on this social media platform.

DealRay

DealRay is a travel discount alert platform that customers are able to use in order to find deals to some of their top vacation choices. This company was able to used destination focused video advertising on Instagram in order to educate and catch the attention of their followers and potential followers on Instagram. With the help of the Instagram tools, DealRay was able to increase their customer acquisitions by 10 percent and over a period of six months, they say an increase in their revenues by five times what they were seeing before.

DealRay was started in 2014 by people who consider themselves travel fanatics. It is a site that is able to combine the power of world-class engineering with a team of travel experts to help travelers and vacationers find the best deals on their travel plans. These deals are then going to be served out to their members; the members are then going to pay a monthly fee in order to get mobile alerts about the deals through a push notification or a text message.

To help them stand out on the busy news feeds of Instagram, DealRay decided that they wanted to use the slideshow feature in order to create some high-quality videos. The adverts were able to feature a beautiful and professional picture of a specific local that they were promoting with a low price that overlaid it. This price was something that members of DealRay were actually able to pay to visit that destination and that price was then compared to the original expensive airfare that others were paying to get there.

To help this company reach the widest audience of potential followers possible, DealRay wanted to keep the targeting they did pretty broad. It chose to target both genders who were between the ages of 18 and 44.

These advertisements were pretty simple to make, but they were intriguing and they had the power to encourage potential customers to share the deals with friends, even if they chose not to use it for themselves. Since these advertisements were intriguing and easy to share, this helped the company to reach more audience than ever before, ensuring that they reached as many people and got more members than they could have done in any other way.

In addition, this site decided to work with the Adverts Manager tool through Instagram to help them keep track of how many conversions came from these advertisements. They then found that in addition to the adverts being shared and viewed thousands of times, they were also the main reason that they saw such a big push in customer acquisitions. For them, it was a spike of 10 percent each week that they did these advertisements.

Watcha Play

This is a streaming service from South Korea. They choose to work with Instagram and do a split test (or

A/B testing) during a holiday period in order to see how effective ads on Instagram Stories would be at helping them to increase how many installs they got for the ad and whether there was a higher awareness of their brand. After doing this split test, they found that they were able to reach 23 percent more people during the test and then they also achieved a 47 percent lower cost for each app that was installed.

Watcha Play is a video-on-demand streaming and subscription service that comes from South Korea. It is focused on providing its customers with an entertainment experience that is customized and unlike anything that they can get somewhere else. Since this brand is driven by performance, they are always looking for ways to boost their marketing efforts in the most efficient manner possible.

To help this company optimize their digital campaigns, they decided to do a split test that was focused mostly on the impact that the Instagram Stories feature on Instagram would have on their ad performance. The overall goal for them was to reach a bigger audience while lowering the costs for everyone.

This particular split test was set up to use two

campaigns. The first on displayed the created ads in the traditional Facebook News Feed along with the Audience Network and the Instagram Feed. Then the second was placed in Instagram Stories as well as with the other three platforms from before.

These ads were a bit different because they featured movie quizzes. As the followers answered the questions, they would be directed to a landing page that could reveal the answers and then talked about what the company did. All the ads were designed so that they would work well on mobile and there were customizations to make them do well on each platform.

This company decided to run each campaign during the Chuseok Thanksgiving holiday for a total of 11 days between September and October 2018. The targeting that they used was pretty broad, including some people who already subscribed to the service, to ensure that they were able to reach the largest audience possible and boost its presence during this time.

At the end of it all, Watcha Play found that when they included these Instagram Stories into their advertising, it helped them to reach 23 percent more people than the other method, but it also helped them to achieve a lower cost for each install of the app; in fact, this cost was 46 percent. In fact, using the Instagram Stories provided a return on investment that was 2.2 times higher compared to the other option.

Virgin Media

The next company we are going to take a look at is Virgin Media. In order to attract excitement and more votes for awards during the BAFTA TV Awards, Virgin Media decided to use Instagram Stories in order to run some ads that were carousel videos. What they found in the end is that this helped them get 42 percent more votes when compared to some of the other channels that they tried out.

First, Virgin Media is a company that is found in Britain and will provide internet, V, and phone services throughout the United Kingdom. Each year, they sponsor the BAFTA Awards show, which allows them to honor both the best international and British contributions to TV from the past year.

Virgin Media decided that they wanted to run a campaign several times, hitting on the four main stages of this awards process. These four stages included the voting, pre-awards, awards night, and then the wrap-up. The reason that they wanted to do this was to help warm up the audience for this and ensure that they could get more people involved and engaged not just during, but before and after the show as well.

Virgin Media is actually considered the first of the telco companies to use this carousel format on Instagram with an objective for generating more leads. They wanted to create ad that was engaging and entertaining so they worked with several agencies including RAPP and Manning Gottlieb OMD in order to come up with a series of mini-episodes that showed the BAFTA ambassador. During these visitors, they urged viewers to swipe up in order to vote for the Must See Moment for this awards show.

Of course, this would keep going after the show was over. Virgin Media kept all of the conversations going simply by making sure that they shared lots of content that they felt would resonate the best with their audiences.

At the end of this campaign, the company saw that they had received a ton of great results. This campaign attracted a lot more interaction when compared to some of the other channels that they chose to work with. For example, the carousel ended up with 42 percent more votes compared to the other channels and it cost them 70 percent less per vote in the process. The company also found that they were able to reduce the amount that they spent on the ads by a total of 39 percent with the help of this ad format compared to what they did in 2017 with their marketing.

Ted Baker

Ted Baker, a fashion brand, decided to run a new campaign using the Instagram platform in order to increase customer awareness of a new collection they were releasing. What happened is that the campaign led to an 8.2 point lift in ad recall from customers.

Ted Baker is a luxury clothing company in Britain that focuses on menswear, womenswear, and various accessories. The brand has stores that are found in the United States and in the United Kingdom and they have been known for some time because of colors and patterns that are very distinctive.

To help them promote a new collection for fall and winter, this company decided to create eight vertical videos, all of which were less than ten seconds long. They then decided to use Instagram Stories to show these videos. All of the videos were showing items from the womenswear and menswear ranges.

The company did take it a bit further from here though. In addition to these ads that were placed in Instagram Stories, there were ads that focused more on the product and they were released in collection and carousel formats from Instagram. These advertisements were designed to encourage consumers to visit the website. They were particularly interested in the consumers who had at one point or another interacted with the campaign, such as seeing the short videos from before, or who had taken the time to visit the Ted Baker website in the past.

These videos were a hit. The customers enjoyed seeing a quick glimpse of the collection and there were many different effects, including kaleidoscopic visuals, split screens, and borders that kept things interesting. In the womenswear campaign, there were a lot of different patterns including exotic animals, florals, and more, and the menswear showcased products that were colorful that were held against a concrete backdrop. Both of the campaigns were done in various homes and even on rooftops around London.

This campaign was a big success for the company. In fact, it resulted in an 8.2 point lift in ad recall and there was also a consideration lift of 3 points. In addition, the campaign resulted in a 22 percent increase in website conversions for the 18 to 24 age range when compared to the spring and summer season they had just finished with.

Ashy Bines

Ashy Bines is known as a fitness brand located on Instagram. This company decided that they wanted to use the feature of Instagram Stories in order to promote the launch of a new app for the company. What happened is that there were almost 13,000 installs of the app in the time of the campaign and these installs occurred at a lower cost per install compared to the projections the company had originally come out with.

Ashy Bines is a personal trainer and fitness brand from Australia. They recently launched a brand new app that had the goal to help women make choices that are healthier. The app is built on an idea of encouraging and empowering women because it helps them to connect to other people who are like-minded and who are interested in losing weight and getting healthier at the same time.

As a part of their strategy to gain more growth, Ashy Bines decided to invest heavily in what is known as their Squad app. Because the demographics of this app are women between the ages of 18 and 35, the brand says that they should work with Instagram Stories as a key platform in order to engage their audience and to get as many install numbers as they can.

Using Ashy Bines as a protagonist, the campaign video had her swiping up to show potential customers what they should do in order to install the app. And it was all done through Instagram Stories. The video was short and sweet, but it got the point across and it helped customers and consumers take a look at the new app and decide if it was the right one for them.

The main goal of this campaign was to drive up the number of installs that occurred with their target audience. The brand decided that these ads needed to be targeted in females, all between the ages of 18 and 64, who were interested in milk and coffee on Instagram. This brand then decided to target the ads to a mixture of worldwide and local audiences that looked like the audience they had just chosen.

The campaign took place over a three-week time period and the results were pretty impressive. For example, this campaign alone, in just three weeks, ended up reaching 4.4 million people throughout the world. The number of app installs was at almost 13,000 and the cost for each install was three times lower than what the company had originally set as their target for this.

Paysafecard

This next business is a prepaid payments company who decided to use Instagram Stories for their marketing as well. This company decided to use this feature in order to reach their audience of gamers during a time when they were having a major sale during the summer. This led to more searches for a sales outlet for the payment card and they were able to do this at a lower price than other similar channels. Paysafecard is a company that is operating in more than 46 countries right now. It is meant to be a simple and secure method for making payments ahead of time. Customers are able to make their purchases online with this payment method, without needing a credit card or a bank account in order to get the payment done. This helps customers keep their information safe, even when they decide to shop online.

The sales for video games during the summer are huge and it is a great time to reach the gaming audience if you want to engage with them. Because of this, Paysafecard decided that they wanted to do a campaign on Instagram that was aimed just at gamers for this one. The ads were all targeted to women and men who were in the age range of 16 to 30 and they were located in Mexico and Europe. To help them narrow down the audience even more, the company decided that the ads should be targeted to individuals who were interested in just a few games, such as Final Fantasy, PUBG, and Dota 2.

In addition to the steps above, Paysafecard decided

that they wanted to do a bit of retargeting. In the processes, they did a few ads that went straight to their website visitors and a lookalike audience based on those same visitors as well. This helped them to reach a larger audience of people who already visited their website and those who may be interested in the services in the future.

The campaign decided to feature some ads that were in a meme like format. The advertisements showed a Paysafecard that was inside an emergency box. Along with this was some copy that urged the customers to break the glass in order to get ahold of the summer sale they were often. This was attention grabbing, allowed the customer to interact with the ad, and reinforced the idea that the company wanted of them being the tool that was needed to help protect their customers.

The campaign was not a long one and only lasted for about a week and a half. In that short amount of time, this company saw a lot of great results. To start, the click-through rate with Instagram Stories was two times higher than what they say with some of their other campaign ad placements on other sites. In addition, they experienced a cost per conversion on these ads that was 76 percent lower than what the company annually paid on average. They also saw that the campaign, in less than two weeks, led to 6000 new internet searches for a sales outlet for the company.

These are just a few of the different examples and case studies of what other companies have been able to do with the help of Instagram advertising. Most of them decided to utilize either split testing or Instagram Stories to help get their message across. Even though all of them come from different backgrounds, different parts of the world, and sell different items, they all saw tremendous success even over short campaigns, and the cost was lower than what they experienced in the past with other channels such as Facebook and Twitter.

What this means is that your business is able to get the same results a well. As long as you can create good content on your profile and build up your followers, you can use all of the features that come with Instagram to reach new customers and make sales, at a fraction of the cost that you can with other traditional methods. It may take a little planning, but what marketing strategy doesn't, to come up with the right target market, the right content to put in the ads, and the right budget, but you are sure to see some great results when you work with advertising on Instagram just like these other companies did as well!

Conclusion

Thank you for making it through to the end of *Instagram Marketing Secrets*. Let's hope it was informative and able to provide you with all of the tools you need to achieve your goals whatever they may be.

The next step is to get started with creating your own Instagram Business Account. Setting up one of these accounts is easy to do and it allows you to get ahold of some of the best features that Instagram has to offer. It is simple to use, allows you to post and look at analytics for your posts, and even makes it easy to work on Instagram Stories and reach your customers in new and exciting ways.

This guidebook took some time to go through all of the different things that you need to know in order to get started with marketing your business on Instagram. We look at the different features that are available for marketers, how to reach your followers in an organic and friendly manner.

When you are done with this guidebook, you will take your Instagram account from brand new to one that has a lot of followers and leads to some great sales for you. When you are ready to see how far your reach can go and the heights that your business can get to, make sure to check out this guidebook to learn more about Instagram marketing.

Finally, if you found this book useful in any way, a review on Amazon is always appreciated!

66253619R00165

Made in the USA
Middletown, DE
06 September 2019